HOW TO MAKE SURE YOUR MONEY LASTS AS LONG AS YOU DO!

A 5% Cash Flow in a 1% Economy

ROBERT E. GRACE
JD, CLU, ChFC, CFEd®, RFC

WORD ASSOCIATION PUBLISHERS
www.wordassociation.com
1.800.827.7903

Published 2012.

Printed in the United States of America.

ISBN: 978-1-59571-772-6
Library of Congress Control Number: 2012931838

Designed and published by

Word Association Publishers
205 Fifth Avenue
Tarentum, Pennsylvania 15084

www.wordassociation.com
1.800.827.7903

"To know and not to do is not to know."

Confucius

"Buying stocks or bonds is gambling. You're betting on prices - you're betting on buying them from those who don't know how much they're worth and selling them to somebody who thinks they're worth more. That's speculation and its short term. It's influenced and driven by supply and demand, and not by the worth of those companies whose value lies underneath that stock price."

John Bogle
Founder and former CEO of the Vanguard Group
June 2009

"You can't invest your way to retirement, you've got to save your way to retirement."

Gary Shilling, *Economist*
September 2009

Table of Contents

Acknowledgments

I would like to dedicate this book to all of my many clients who have been so trusting and loyal over the years, and particularly to my wife Rose. She has given me the support and the encouragement to reach the levels of success that I have in the retirement planning business. This book is written with all my love for my four children Bob, Jr., Erin, Kevin, and Heather.

Thanks to Randy Hammon for sharing his insight and statistics that made this book possible.

Also my acknowledgements would not be complete without recognizing the talented team of staff members at Grace Advisory Group: Tax and Retirement Specialists who consistently provide support and insight into the creative design of retirement plans that provide safety, tax reduction, increased income, and reduction or elimination of retirement planning fees for our clients.

And finally to David Callanan, Cody Foster, Derek Thompson, Josh Whitehead, Damon Thompson, and all the wonderful supportive and creative team at Advisors Excel who so effectively facilitate the sharing of ideas amongst the superb advisory professionals who are members of their elite team.

Prologue

If you're like most of my clients, you've worked hard all your life. You've saved and sacrificed, and grown a sizable retirement fund as a result. Now, however, the future doesn't look so certain. Many of you have seen as much as 40% of your retirement fund disappear in a matter of months. And it's *not* because you were unlucky or uninformed. It's because you're still operating in paycheck mode, as you have most of your life, when what's required is a shift in perspective.

There are three phases of money: accumulation, preservation, and distribution. The first phase, accumulation, is what I call workday "paycheck mode." The paycheck is what puts food on your plate, clothes on your back, and gas in your tank. Taking investment risks does not affect your lifestyle during the paycheck phase. When the market goes up, your broker or advisor calls to say, "Look what a great job I did for you!" When it goes down (and it always does at some point), you call your broker who, if he takes your call, says, "I don't have any control over the market. But hang in there - it'll come back eventually."

I don't care who your financial advisor is - last time I checked, nobody had a crystal ball that works! Even if your advisor talked as though he or she could look into the future, we all know they can't. Most brokers infer that the past has some connection with the future. It's fundamental to their investment philosophy; they're constantly hawking the story of historical returns. The question I pose to you is: What connection does yesterday actually have with tomorrow? The answer is: none at all. The darling of Wall Street today probably won't be the darling tomorrow ... and it certainly won't be the darling in five years. That's the fallacy of investing in the casino.

The story your advisor or broker wanted you to believe said that the market would climb back out of that hole and continue to go up. In years past, that might have been true. But those were the years you had plenty of something that's not so abundant today if you are close to or in retirement … time.

When you've got that paycheck coming in, you can wait for the market to go back up. But now that you're retired, things are different. That workday paycheck no longer exists, and you still need cash flow. We call it your "retirement paycheck." If you maintain your investments in stocks and bonds, your money is at the whim of the market—it might go up one month and down the next. I don't know anybody who wants to eat one month and starve the next!

During our working and investment years, most of us use a process called "dollar cost averaging." This system says that if you put an equal amount of money in an investment on a very regular basis, buying some of the assets high and some low and averaging the costs in the middle, then if you sell any stocks, bonds, or mutual funds above the middle or mean price, you'll make a profit on the total portfolio. When times are good, it's not a bad investment philosophy.

However, if you try to do that on withdrawal, it's called reverse dollar cost averaging, and it works just as effectively on a negative basis. If you are pulling a fixed amount of money out of an asset that goes up and down, you are going to reduce your total account value fast. Too fast.

Once you retire, the pot of money you've spent the last forty years putting together has to last you the rest of your life. It wasn't so long ago that people retired at sixty-five and died at sixty-five and a half. They didn't need much of a plan! But today people are living well into their nineties and sometimes over age one hundred. I recently heard an expert on aging say that there are people alive today who will live to be a hundred and fifty years old. With longevity on the rise, you need a plan that absolutely contractually guarantees income for as long as you live, not just as long as the money lasts.

Income is the only important thing in retirement. It's not net worth. It's not the number at the bottom of your financial statement. It's what's coming in the front door to put food on your plate, gas in your tank, and clothes on your back—and hopefully all the additional perks of the good life you've worked so hard to enjoy in retirement.

So how do you create retirement income? By finding the right retirement professionals to help you design the best possible retirement plan, in writing, created by an experienced team, including a group of highly credentialed retirement planning specialists, CPAs, and attorneys.

How do you find these professionals? You can flip open the Yellow Pages. You can search on Google. You can talk to your friends or family. You can get free advice from your next door neighbor, which is of course the most dangerous kind of advice there is. You might have a neighbor on one side who is very intelligent—a professor or a physician. Maybe your neighbor on the other side is a plumber. Most likely, the plumber makes more money than the physician or professor! But the point is: when they give you advice on a topic that is not their main expertise, it's going to be the most expensive advice you will ever get. Beware of free advice—everyone has a bias.

Instead, find someone with the proper credentials, education, and experience. Look for designations like CFP (Certified Financial Planner), ChFC (Chartered Financial Consultant), CLU (Chartered Life Underwriter), RFC (Registered Financial Consultant), and CFEd (Certified Financial Educator). All of these designations require numerous courses involving hours of study and very difficult tests.

Also, look for people who are multi-disciplinary. Ideally, you want to find a team with people on staff from both sides of the coin: Wall Street and the fixed side (the insurance industry). They should have experience and financial training on both sides, not just cursory knowledge of one or the other. Most stock brokers will tell you they know about annuities, and most annuity salespeople will tell you they know all about stocks and bonds and mutual funds. Don't believe it. Generally speaking, each side knows very little about the other. But if you can find the rare, talented, and experienced individual who has been certified, educated, and licensed in both areas, you're more likely to get an unbiased opinion as to the proper choices for your retirement account.

At Grace Advisory Group: Tax and Retirement Specialists, we're lucky to have a team compiled of just those individuals. We truly are the best! And it's our job to figure out how best to ensure a guaranteed lifetime retirement income for you.

As you read this book, remember to keep an open mind. There are going to be some new ideas we'll be presenting that hopefully allow you to find peace of mind, security, and safety in your golden years. We'll show you strategies that allow you to do exactly what you want to do in retirement.

When asked about their financial goals, most retirees' say they would like to lower their taxes, as well as increase their income now and in the future because of inflationary needs. They want to reduce (or better yet, eliminate) any of the fees they may be paying for competent financial advice. And above all else, they want to make their money safe.

I've worked with thousands of retirees and people on the brink of retiring, and when I ask them whether they prefer risk or safety, the overwhelming majority of them choose safety and leading experts agree. The older they get, the more safety they want. When you are young, you have time to regenerate any losses that occur in risk based investing. I'm sure I don't have to tell you that the one thing we don't have as much of as we get older is that ever-elusive asset … time. What that means is that you have to change the style of investing that you do in retirement as opposed to what you did during the paycheck years.

There is no such thing as a little bit of risk or a little bit of safety. Saying, "I'm in just in a little bit of risk," is on par with saying, "I'm just a little bit pregnant"! I don't mean to offend anyone; I simply mean, you either are or you aren't. Risk is risk, and safety is safety. It's either there or it isn't.

Retirement should be about safety and it should be about guarantees. My forty-three years of experience tells me that the only reason people take risk at all is because they feel they have to—to get a competitive rate of return on their investments or their money. As we'll discuss later in the book, taking risks is not necessarily required in order to get competitive, safe, consistent returns. It's the financial version of the fable about the tortoise and the hare. The "tortoise"—a long, consistent, only going up account—will beat the volatility of ups and downs in the market every time.

Before we begin, I want to briefly share a few of the most common questions we hear from our clients.

- Is my money safe?
- What financial instruments are the best for retirement?

- How can I hang on to the money I currently have?
- Are my current investments safe?
- Am I going to have enough money to sustain me and my spouse for both of our lifetimes?
- How do I ensure I have access to cash flow during retirement?
- How can I lower my taxes and thereby keep more of my money?
- Will I have enough money to maintain my current lifestyle during my retirement?
- Will there be anything leftover for the kids?
- Will I be able to keep up with inflation?

Do any of these hit home for you? If yes, we're not surprised. If not, they should. Every American should be worrying about all of these questions, both pre- and post-retirement. These are the questions I've set out to answer in this book.

So how is it that you protect your money? What techniques are available and what should you do? In *How to Make Sure Your Money Lasts As Long As You Do!*, we'll be talking about the many ways to ensure that you never run out of money. I'll show you how to make sure you are getting a good enough return to maintain a good lifestyle—not one that is less than you had when you worked, but as good if not better.

Get ready to "Retire with Grace"!

chapter one

Now What?

They stole your future.

We all know who "they" are. Wall Street—the same people who told you, for all those years, that your money would be safe with them, that it would grow, and that if you played by the rules, you'd have all the money you needed when you needed it—for your children's education, for retirement, for that trip around the world.

You went on a trip, all right. Wall Street took you for a ride. That was your trip.

I'm not writing to you if you're a day trader, a gambler, a get-rich-quick kind of person, a penny stock lover, or someone who invests in every crazy scheme that comes on late-night infomercials. If those people lost everything, it really serves them right. That's not investing; that's gambling.

I'm not writing to the super wealthy whose lifestyle will not be affected if they lost 20% of their money in the Wall Street casino. Although, if the super wealthy aren't smart enough to control and secure the majority of their hard-earned money, I may be talking to them. There's nothing sadder than seeing wealth earned by the fruit of one's labor and expertise disappear in a risky endeavor outside one's expertise and control. And it happens all the time!

You're different. You've played by all the rules. You've worked hard all your life, scrimped and saved, lived on a budget, postponed gratification, and put money aside every month. Wall Street told you to put your money in the stock market and stay in it for the long haul, and you followed the advice of the so-called experts. You did your homework. You picked the investments for your IRA, 401(k) or 403(b) plan, or other retirement plan that made the most sense in building your retirement nest egg. You allocated your assets, you weighed risks, and you thought you were taking the prudent course.

And look where it got you. Decades of investing and doing the right thing ... wiped out in just a few horrible months. Now you don't even want to open your statements.

Your retirement ... gone.

Your savings ... decimated.

Your trust … violated.

Your concerns and fears about the future … magnified beyond anything you could have imagined.

You were looking at retiring—maybe selling the house, taking the equity, and doing something you've always dreamed of. You fantasized about moving to Hawaii or some other dream location. Or maybe you'd just stay put, watch your grandchildren grow up, and help your kids from time to time with your money and time. Now your financial future has been shattered.

So the question arises: *Now what?* And that's the question this book seeks to answer. What do you do now? Whom do you trust? Where do you invest? How do you get made whole again? And how could this whole financial meltdown have happened in the first place?

If you want to learn how to grow your money safely, even in these turbulent, almost unprecedented economic times, I'll show you how to do so in this book. Want to get rich quick? Hit on the next hot penny stock? Ride the wave of the latest easy money scheme somebody's peddling on an infomercial at 2 a.m.? Want me to compete with the financial network's talking heads, who didn't steer you to safety several years ago, even when they sensed things were heading over a cliff? Again, if you answered "yes" to any of those questions, then I'm not your guy.

If you desire to understand what really happened, why the key investment vehicles that Wall Street put you in were doomed to failure practically from the start, and above all *what to do now*, then come along for this journey. I'll give you a philosophy of investing and a strategy for going forward that Wall Street will never tell you about because if you've got safe money, they can't steal it from you. And that's what this book is all about.

Set Realistic Financial Goals

So how did we get in this mess in the first place?

When it comes to the way money changes hands between the individual investor and brokerage houses, I imagine Jack Nicholson delivering a line from Edward Winslow's book *Blind Faith*: "Well, the broker made money and the firm made money—and two out of three ain't bad."

Let's say an average investor—we'll call him Fred—sees a full-page ad in the newspaper about some innovative strategy of investing. He calls the number or visits the website to sign up and attends the seminar. What happens next? To paraphrase William Bernstein's writing in *The Intelligent Asset Allocator*, if Fred gains some knowledge and continues to do his own research and pick his own stocks, then *he doesn't know that he doesn't know*. What's Fred not grasping? He doesn't see how Wall Street makes money on his every move. Whether Fred's stock pick goes up, down, or sideways, the Wall Street casino cashes in.

What happens if Fred gives his money to a so-called "investment professional"? Now the money is in the hands of someone, in Bernstein's words, "who indeed knows that he or she doesn't know, but whose livelihood depends on them *appearing* to know." In other words, the financial advisors at Stocks 'R' Us know enough to get you to put money with them, but their knowledge about your investment choices is severely limited; they don't have complete access to the accuracy of the information received from their analysts. And what they don't know affects you. The consequences of their actions in peddling Wall Street's constant misinformation will leave you holding the bill.

Fred, like the rest of us, is an innocent bystander who gave his money over to people who know little more than he does about investments! They know a lot about the process of *selling you* an investment, but they don't know much about the true worth of those investments, the risk level, and whether you should be buying them in the first place. So Fred, thinking he's about to take a walk down Easy Street, actually finds himself run over by an armored truck taking his money—and the money of all the other Freds of the world—to the Wall Street vault.

Finance gurus on CNBC, MSNBC, and other financial shows advised people to invest for the long run, implying that no matter how much money people lose today, they'd earn it back in the future. In January 1999, the S&P 500 Index read 1229; ten years later in 2009, it stood at 1000—an 18% decline. The numbers show that the S&P has not progressed much in the past decade. We might have another large drop ahead—we don't know. Somebody might have put their nest egg into the market a decade ago, only to see it drop as much as 40 to 50% at the bottom of the current market in early 2009. Even after the stock market improvements since March 2009, as of this writing, the general S&P 500 Stock Index is STILL lower than its January 2000 level.

At the same time, CDs, fixed annuities, and US treasury bonds have proven secure—not sexy but secure. They grew at an average rate of 4% annually over the last ten years. People who held them are significantly ahead of those who did not. Ten years ago, an advisor would have said that investing in CDs, annuities, and treasury bonds was a stupid mistake. Today, a whole lot of people wish they had made that very mistake!

The strangest thing is that all this has happened before. After the crash of 1929, it took until 1954 for investors to get back to the breakeven level on the Dow Jones Industrial Average. I know that sounds hard to believe, but it's true. If your grandfather lost his savings when the market crashed in October 1929, it would have taken him twenty-five full years before his investments returned to that level of the Dow.

If you don't believe me, look at the numbers. Numbers are your friend! The Dow peaked at 384 in late September 1929. A year later, in September 1930, it had slumped to 194, a 46% drop. By September 1931, in the bear market recovery, it went back to 283—a 46% rebound. However, Grandpa was still down 26% from the market peak in September 1929. Then, in July 1932, the Dow crashed to 41 ... and that's not a typo! It went all the way down to 41. Even after a five-year gain of 385% between 1932 and 1937, the market only scratched back to 194, still 50% below the September 1929 high of 384.

Does this sound eerily similar to what happened a couple of years ago? Just add a few zeroes to the Dow index number, and it's déjà vu all over again. The Dow peaked in October 2007 at 14,066. It dropped ... and dropped ... and dropped ... until it had reached 8,000 in October 2008—a 43% decrease. By March 2009, the Dow had dropped more to 6,440, a 54% plunge from its October 2007 peak, wiping out trillions of dollars of wealth—including, very possibly, much of *your* wealth.

Are you starting to see a similar historical pattern developing? In the stock market, it's the 1930s all over again. Disaster, followed by government intervention and hype, followed by a false recovery based on nothing but wishful thinking and Wall Street hype, and followed by the reality check resulting in …

If you can't tell me what follows and you're betting your retirement future on that guess in the stock market, I would call you a gambler and your advisor a bookie! The bottom line is you can't afford to lose money. We'll get more deeply into this later on, but here's the first takeaway I want to share with you: ***A loss is much worse for you than a gain is good.***

In light of the demonstrated history of losses, how is it that Wall Street keeps getting people to invest? <u>By creating a false impression of security based on a false notion of expertise</u>, that's how. If they can make you feel safe and that they absolutely know what they're talking about, you'll hand over your cash to them. That's the secret of their success.

As an investor, you must keep an especially sharp eye out for false impressions of security. One way to do that is to watch out when financial advisors start throwing out the names of celebrities or famous investors who own the stocks or investments they're pitching. Is there substance behind the pitch, or is it just another commercial or infomercial with a celebrity endorsement? A well-known name is often thrown out to increase the credentials of a risky investment. Such is the case when advisors say in order to get someone interested that Warren Buffett is buying this stock or Bill Gates is looking to acquire this company.

There are consequences for not investigating the fundamentals behind mass fanfare for a stock. Back in the technology bubble from 1997 to 2000, some companies had zero earnings per share and no sales, but their stock was selling for $100 per share. Even an established company like Broadcom went from $9 in 1997 to over $170 at the top of the market in mid-2000. Remember when AOL ruled the Internet? Despite a number of growing threats, shares skyrocketed to over $100 in 1998.

Yet when the bubble burst, those prices plummeted… and still haven't recouped. As of 2009, companies such as AOL, which was once selling at $100 per share, have dipped down to below $20. Nobody's buying the stock now, even at that low price. Investors finally got fed up with the continued misinformation from the bookies on Wall Street. You might as well have invested at a craps table at a Vegas hotel; at least that way, they might have given you a few free drinks or a shot at the buffet for your troubles.

During this same time, the NASDAQ stock index, which is comprised mostly of technology stocks, was at 4575 in January 2000—today, after the stock market recovery from March 2009 to the time of this writing in late 2011, the NASDAQ is still down 44% from its January 2000 level. Is this the way you want to plan for your retirement?

When people talk about limits today, there's often a negative connotation. But when I use the word *limits*, I don't mean it in a negative way. My definition of limit has to do with "comfort zone" or "what you can handle comfortably and effectively in life."

The reason people get scammed and make mistakes, such as choosing the wrong major in college or going after the wrong career, is that they fail to recognize their limits. Maybe they lacked someone in their lives who would help set parameters for them. In other words, no one sat down and helped them outline their beliefs, goals, passions, and limits—no one gave them that reality check, if you will.

Wall Street really likes to tell people to look at where they should be compared with other successful investors as if it were possible to obtain everything imaginable simply by playing a game of compare and contrast. This message is completely unrealistic; yet people keep buying into it. Is this the way you want to plan for your retirement?

The truth is that different skill levels and economic backgrounds create better opportunities and career choices for some people than for others, but a lot of people want to believe that all they have to do to change their fortune is dream big. I believe in big dreams … but in order to achieve them, you have to "wake up" from the nightmare created by Wall Street. It's time to start working on *your* dreams—not theirs!

That's why it's so important to keep an eye on your realistic limits. When a financial advisor comes along and tells you that he can make more money for you than what you are making right now, you have to ask realistic questions about what happens if he doesn't. When you walk into a Vegas casino, you should know how much you're willing, or how much you can afford, to lose. The same is true when you enter the Wall Street casino. You have to examine who you are, what you make, and what your goals are. Is it really possible to get an annual return of 10 to 20% on your investments over a ten to twenty-year period?

In my role as financial advisor, I often meet prospective clients who say, "My current broker is promising me annual returns of 10%. Can you match that?" I tell them, "No, but I'll give you my best long shot in the fifth race at the Florida Derby!" In all seriousness, I would be honest and give an answer based on reality. There's nothing real about getting 10% a year risk-free. The brokers may be getting great returns on your money—but you won't.

The problem with many advisors is that they do not set parameters for their clients. They can't constantly put more and more money in the market and hope that the market will comply; they need to know when enough is enough. Investors don't need to know earnings per share; they need to know their own level of contentment. How much do you really need to be happy? Do you need all the money in the world? And are you willing to risk everything you already have to get that extra piece of the pie? Or do you have enough right now to live decently with enough in your investment portfolio so you can retire and live decently later on?

Investors need to remember that all objects of hope should be based on some sort of substantiated fact. That requires asking questions like the following: What is my current budget? How will I pay off college loans for my kids? Where do I want to live when I retire? How do I worry less about what is going to come later in life and enjoy life now so that when I get to my goals, my spouse is there with me instead of her divorce attorney? Parameters need to be set. And if your financial advisor hasn't set parameters, find a new one.

I'm not necessarily saying that your advisor or broker is crooked. Plenty of them are upstanding men and women. They just might not have the knowledge required to make the best decisions with your money.

It's like a dentist. You go to the same dentist for years, and they do a good job cleaning, drilling, and filling. But all of a sudden you need an implant. You ask your dentist, "Do you do implants?"

"Well," they say, "I can. I don't do a lot of them—mainly I do crowns and fillings. But sure, I'll give it a whirl."

Do you want that person doing your implant? Probably not! You want to go to the specialist, the guy or gal who all they do is implants. Don't you want them doing yours?

It's the same with your finances. If you have the opportunity to go to a specialist, why would you choose anything but?

Avoid Financial Fallout

When betting on sports and on the floor of the New York Stock Exchange, knowledge is power. There's a huge imbalance of power in the financial markets. To put it simply, they have all the knowledge … and all the power … and you have none. They never tell you that. Why should they?

Every time Fred, or anyone else, signs an agreement on the application to create a brokerage account, there's one sentence in the fine print that Fred doesn't notice and that his broker will *never* highlight. It's a disclaimer that can be summarized as follows: "We want to bring to your attention that there is a *potential conflict of interest* in our financial advice to you. We help raise money, do the initial public offerings, and underwrite for the very companies in which we are advising you to invest. We are going to try to not let this relationship sway us, but there is no guarantee."

Every single investor with every single brokerage house signs an application that contains a clause like this. Every single investor—all the Freds of the world—are unknowingly giving their stockbroker *permission* to allow a possible conflict of interest that could steal their future dreams.

So whose interest is most important to the brokerage house? Is it Fred's? Fred may have an account with $50,000, or even $500,000, in it. That's a lot of money to Fred, but it's a drop in the bucket compared to the fees and discounted stock prices that the brokerage houses receive from the companies they are pimping. (And I use that word intentionally, by the way.) Do you think they'll ever reveal to Fred any negative information about the companies whose stocks they are recommending? Of course not! That's because the broker-salesman doesn't know the entire story.

For a Wall Street brokerage house, the corporate finance entities typically come first, and the retail brokerage division comes second in fees generated and fortunes created for their executives. In essence, the executives of the brokerage houses and their corporate clients are reaping windfalls while the public is getting advice that is not always in its best financial interest. Guess who's left holding the bag?

Indeed, executives of major corporations are making incredibly large sums of money that you never hear about. Maybe you're old enough to remember the early 1980s when Chrysler was on the verge of bankruptcy, and the company stock was down to just $3 per share. The head of Chrysler at the time, Lee Iacocca, went to Congress and basically said: "Give us a billion dollars in loan guarantees so that we can function, or I'm going to bankrupt the company and you will have to pay $1.5 billion for our pension plan." So Congress made what seemed like the prudent decision at the time and bailed out Chrysler for $1 billion.

I know Iacocca is considered one of the great American financial heroes, but unfortunately, there's more to the story. He didn't just save jobs—he made himself a fortune. Iacocca accepted a salary, after the government bailout, of $1 per year. But Iacocca also owned stock options as the top Chrysler executive, probably in the $3 to $5 per share range. After the bailout—after taxpayers footed the bill for Chrysler's recovery—the price of

Chrysler's stock soared to $48 a share within seven years. Iacocca made millions and millions of dollars by exercising his stock options, a fact that the American people never knew about. Did taxpayers share in that windfall? Of course not! Iacocca was a hero, all right—to his accountant, his family, and his estate.

Ever since, CEOs have looked at the Iacocca story and asked one simple question: "Where's mine?" And the pay of top executives has skyrocketed ever since to levels that are truly obscene. I don't mind seeing people being highly compensated for a job well done. But do these guys really deserve hundreds of millions of dollars—even as they drive their companies into the ground? I certainly don't think so. And guess who's paying for all that salary? Look in the mirror, Mr. or Ms. Taxpayer. They get rich because of your willingness to trust them with your money, and they don't even send you thank you notes. Imagine how cramped their hands would get having to write to millions of Freds all over the country—indeed, all over the world—thanking you for your tax contributions to their astonishing wealth.

The story of Lee Iacocca and the Chrysler bailout is relevant today more than ever. Newly hired executives have been approved by the government to run banks and Wall Street firms that are just coming out of bankruptcy due to the economic collapse. Fearing public outrage, the compensation of these new executives is closely monitored for excess. While these executives are forbidden to get large salaries and bonuses, it does seem to be more acceptable for them to participate in stock options, if they perform well with taxpayer funds. Believe me—their employers will have no problem skirting regulations and paying them the big bucks.

The executives own company stock as part of their compensation, and they are able to get stock options while the prices are very low. However, the public doesn't know when and how the executives are going to get extra money because the ones at the top have access to information that you don't. They know just when to pull the trigger on their stock options because they know when bad news is coming that will depress the price of the stock. It's legalized insider trading. And the average investors—the Freds of the world—are stuck at the wrong end of the un-level playing field. When you buy a stock (from those in the know), you're guessing. When they sell a stock (to you), they're acting out of solid knowledge that you don't have.

Unless you know what's going on inside the Wall Street firms, it's next to impossible to make as much money as the executives make. The people who make the most money betting the horses are those who got a tip from a jockey or a trainer. By analogy, the people who do well on Wall Street have access to information that the rest of the public does not have. The executives of the corporations and brokerage houses make all the money. The public receives a small piece of the pie after all the management, administrative, and other fees they charge.

There's a perception that the executives of the bailed-out institutions are being paid low salaries, but the public has no idea to what extent these seeming "heroes" are excessively compensated with stock options. If the public knew, there would be more outrage than the executives could handle. So, naturally, the public will never know.

Something else I find outrageous is the way the market *still* tells the average Joe that he can make millions overnight just by investing his life savings in the market. There's an ongoing bombardment of such propaganda as if the market meltdown had never happened. How dumb do they really think we are? For example, you might remember an ad featuring a taxi driver who is also a successful day trader; he only drives a taxi because he owns the taxi company. Then there was the ad showing a wine connoisseur who invested her money in a 401(k) and somehow made enough to buy her own vineyard. The only way she could have made that kind of money would be if she'd invested with Bernie Madoff … and somehow got out before he went bust.

As a result of those ads, people often begin to think that investing is always glamorous and lucrative, and they *don't* think about the risks involved. The message is always, "Look how easy it is to be a stock trader! Even your grocer is making a fortune." The same appeal to greed attracts people to Las Vegas with the same results: You'll always hear the boasts about how much people made, but people never tell the truth about how much money they lost.

People like to feel important, and that sense of self-importance is fueled by their ability to say "*my* advisor" or "*my* attorney" or "*my* broker." So even when their broker is losing money, they'll still praise him and say something like, "He promises me that I'll recover my losses by making me more than 10% a year going forward." Wall Street is trying to provide an environment where people think that easy money can be made no matter the circumstance. They'll do anything to perpetuate the idea that such a place actually exists, until all the people they've conned are practically lying in the gutter, dead broke.

It was no different in real estate. Anyone who has worked in real estate or has owned a house knows that approximately every ten or twelve years, we cycle between bull and bear markets, meaning there's always a chance that house prices will fall. Yet, due to the fear of missing out on the market or the desire to make more money, people refinanced their houses and threw their equity into either the over-priced stock market or into overinflated real estate. Then they refinanced their houses again or sold them in an attempt to make more money with another stock or real estate strategy.

But, as we all know, trees don't grow to the sky. After a decade or so of easy money, some people lost everything they made earlier. How? By buying a house at the top of the market with easy financing from the banks before the downturn came. Now, after the housing market has collapsed, some can't refinance the house they have and some can't buy the same house they sold a decade ago under the new, higher qualification standards. Others can't tap the equity in their homes because banks won't qualify them for home equity lines of credit. Only in retrospect, people ask, "Why didn't anyone point out that there was a major possibility the real estate market would go bust after seeing house prices triple in the past ten years?"

It's a great question. Why didn't anybody try to stop the music? None of the talking heads on MSNBC or CNBC stepped up to say, "Now is the time to be safe and get out of the market" or "It's time to stop playing the real estate game in the midst of a bubble." Why? Because *these networks are funded by Wall Street firms.* Who advertises on them? The Wall Street investment houses. It's a simple case of "whose bread I eat, his song I sing." So much for "impartial" investment advisors. On these networks, the on-air "talents" do nothing more than promote themselves, their services, books, and magazines, or whatever else they have to offer. No one sells anything in a bull market by telling people to get out of the market. And no one wants to hear negative news that would hurt their investment portfolios.

Nobody paid attention to the fact that from 2005 to 2007, many people who couldn't have qualified in the past under prudent underwriting standards were suddenly able to buy a half-million dollar house in a heartbeat with nothing more than a pulse and a false Social Security number. The banks allowed these purchases, and the executives on Wall Street demanded them. Everybody knew. The job of a mortgage portfolio professional in a bank is to package those loans, get them to Wall Street, let others peddle them off to somebody else, and continue the process. Yet no one spoke out about the outrageous activities they witnessed in the markets because they would have lost their jobs. The media "covering" Wall Street was really just *covering up* for Wall Street. Fear and greed ruled once again—the old familiar culprits.

Some people have finally gotten fed up. One of the bestselling financial gurus who for years championed the strategy of the "little guy" investing in stocks has now become a spokeswoman for the FDIC, an organization charged with guaranteeing bank safety. But before her involvement with the FDIC, this woman told investors to stay in the market for the long run no matter what or they wouldn't be able to retire. My response to her is simply to pick one side or the other. It's a choice between gambling and safety. And only now are you telling all those millions of "little guys" you advised to gamble their hard-earned dollars on the stock market to aim for safety and security. Thanks a lot!

The truth is that Wall Street was *never* on your side, even when it was making a fortune off of you. What's mindboggling for me is the fact that many Wall Street firms do not offer adequate downside protection plans for their clients. My stockbroker friends have told me about a strategy that the wealthy clients used for years: If you had a lot of money in the market, you always employed *stock protection options*. For example, you would pay the option premium of a strategy that allowed your broker to sell your stocks if the prices fell below a certain level. As a result, you wouldn't lose beyond 12 to 15% of your investments. Why weren't Mom-and-Pop investors—the little guys—offered this same protection? Probably because their brokers never wanted to raise the ugly possibility that *stocks could go down*.

Over and over again, we've witnessed the irresponsibility that corporate executives display toward shareholders, the public, and regulators. The executives must think that they are above the law because they've gotten away with robbery for so long. What does trust and integrity mean when we see AIG insurance executives spending thousands of taxpayer dollars partying away at the St. Regis Resort in California? What triggered the party? Why the news of AIG's bailout with hundreds of billions of dollars of taxpayer money!

We also have the example of GM and Chrysler executives flying separately in their private jets to plead poverty before Congress when their corporations were on the verge of bankruptcy. How do we define trust when Bernard Madoff, the financier who people and institutions in the top ranks of our society trusted, cheated his investors out of tens of billions of dollars? The SEC was repeatedly tipped that there were major issues with Madoff concerning his investment strategies … but why wasn't a thorough investigation performed?

The reason might have been that there is indeed a good-old-boy network operating on Wall Street. After all, Madoff had a solid reputation as the former chairman of NASDAQ, which meant that he'd had past dealings with the regulatory agencies of Wall Street.

It's no wonder people fell over themselves to invest with Madoff even though insiders on Wall Street and in the government had solid information that he was running a massive scam … and that he had been doing so for years. How else was it possible for him to show 15% annual gains at times when the market was down as much as 40%? But you didn't have to be a friend of Bernie's to get burned. All you had to have was a few extra dollars in your bank account … and a dream.

If we want to dig ourselves out of the ditch we're in and ensure that something like this doesn't happen again, then we need to stop giving over our financial futures to a system based on imperfect knowledge. The brokerage house knows all but doesn't tell all; the investor knows little but hopes for the best. It's like Lucy pulling the football away from Charlie Brown. You'd think that kid would wise up after a while. He doesn't, and as investors, neither do we.

One of my friends often tells me, "I don't want to open the statement from my broker. I don't want to know. My broker told me not to stress out and that the money is going to come back in the long run. I'm not worried." Then my friend always turns to me and asks, "Are you worried?"

I *am* worried! Yes, I am. I am worried about investors not knowing what to do next. I know that deep down my friend is worried too. In order to eliminate the stress, we need to understand the fundamental principles of investing for ourselves, so that we can start controlling our own assets. Our money can only be considered safe money if we know where it is today and where it will be tomorrow. In this book, I want to show you how to keep your money safe.

We as investors have abdicated our responsibility for our finances to others who might not know the basic concepts necessary to do what is best with those finances. The basic concepts are *knowledge, understanding,* and *control.* These concepts are not applied by investors because they don't know, don't understand, or don't control what's going on with their finances. Furthermore, we don't tend to treat our advisors as partners when we should do so. One of the reasons might be intimidation: We're afraid to tell the professionals what to do because we hire them to tell *us* what to do. We say, "Here is the money and I trust you." Things should not be that way. We need to pick our advisors based on how they have protected their clients over the last ten to twenty years … instead of letting them have free reign over our money in the Wall Street casino.

As you read *How to Make Sure Your Money Lasts As Long As You Do!*, I'd like to assist you with your finances by helping you set proper parameters for your financial life. Anyone can develop his or her own strategy of how to handle money by understanding their own core values and what is important to them. A solid future sits on a three-legged stool: finances, relationships, and your health. Take out any one of those legs and the stool will collapse. Your relationships and your health are your business. Your financial success is my responsibility.

I want you to develop a customized strategy unique to your goals and your hopes rather than overloading you with information that does nothing but paralyze your decision-making process. Knowledge is not the issue here. Today thanks to the information explosion on the Internet, you as a solo investor have as many tools to gain knowledge about investments as any stockbroker has. It's all about how you use that information!

Anyone can follow my advice, no matter his or her socioeconomic background. Whether you or your parents went to Yale or jail, this approach will work for you. My dream for you is that you be content, no matter what your current situation. If you can learn to be content with where you are at this time in your life, your finances, your relationships, and your health will do nothing but flourish. Whether you work for the government, in education, law enforcement, the medical field, or in the private sector, I can help you. Together, we'll figure out an answer to that puzzling question, "Now what?"

But first, let me introduce myself. My name is Bob Grace, and I've had over forty-three years of experience in providing estate, retirement, and tax planning for individuals. It is my desire that, as you read this book, you can draw from that experience to create a happier, safer retirement … for *you*.

chapter two

Meet Your Financial Architect

I'm lucky enough to be married to Rose, an exceptionally talented woman who speaks six languages and holds two architect degrees. One of the things Rose has taught me is that I, too, am engaged by my clients as an architect. But I don't deal in building design and structural engineering like she does. I am a financial architect.

When you go to an architect, you tell them what you're looking for in a home.

"I want a Spanish style, two story," you say. "With four bedrooms, three bathrooms, and a three car garage."

So the architect comes back in a month with an initial drawing, and from there, you proceed to tweak their design. You change the location of the doors and windows, adjust the angle of the roof line, and add a laundry room in the back. You collaborate closely with the architect, who continues to redraw the design until it is the exact visual representation of the house of your dreams.

The reason you use an architect is that they know all of the available options. They know there are 155 different styles of windows, 87 kinds of brick, and 212 shades of paint to choose from. Because of the breadth and depth of their knowledge, they can boil it down to a smaller number of options that they feel will be compatible with your style preference and optimal price range. So you sit down with the architect and decide on the Anderson windows, the antique brick, and "vermillion dusk" for the veranda.

A financial architect does exactly the same thing. It's my job and my team's job to sit down with our clients, find out what their financial goals are, what they are trying to accomplish, and what they want the end results to be. Based on how they answer these questions, we design a preliminary plan for their "house of financial security and growth." Once that initial plan is on the table, we meet a second and sometimes even a third and fourth time to continue to hone our plan until we've got it exactly right—the perfect plan to accomplish their goals at the highest level.

While my wife knows floor plans and window types, my team knows financial products and instruments. Our job is to narrow these down so you've got exactly the ones in your portfolio that are right for you.

Many people have tried to "do it themselves" with many things, even their own financial planning. Because of luck or even possibly a degree of astuteness, some have been relatively successful. Like most professional financial advisors, they've focused their efforts, skills, and talents on growing their money, not on protecting and distributing it.

If this describes you, congratulations! You've successfully grown your wealth. But that makes it even more essential, in the retirement planning stage of your financial life, that you have a retirement specialist help create the perfect plan for preservation and distribution. Few people would order a scalpel by mail order and try to do surgery on themselves. So why in the world would you want to design your own plan when you could work with a professional who will make all the potential products, instruments, and strategies available to you, allowing you, with their assistance, to choose the best alternatives to accomplish your financial goals?

Don't do it yourself. If you do, you're looking at a lot of failure and frustration. After all, if you become a slave to your finances during your retirement years, it defeats the whole purpose of retirement! Why not secure financial peace of mind, allowing you to do what you want and like to do? Spend time with the grandkids, travel, play golf, play bridge - do whatever the heck it is you've worked thirty to forty years for, so that in your retirement you can "Retire with Grace."

Have fun, enjoy yourself, and let somebody else help you design a professional plan that's on autopilot. That plan should do the one thing—the *only* thing, in fact—that is important in retirement, and that is to offer a guaranteed lifetime income for you and your spouse and, if you choose, to allow you to pass on assets to your children, grandchildren, or charity.

At Grace Advisory Group: Tax and Retirement Specialists, our knowledge is born of experience. Over the last four decades, we've seen the stock market crash, stabilize, and crash again. We've seen housing bubbles burst and the tech boom flat line. We've watched people invest millions in mutual funds and the bond market, and we've watched them lose more than half of it when things go bad. We've also seen our clients *maintain* their wealth, enjoying a rich and fulfilling life while everyone around them is floundering.

How do they do it? I'll tell you. But first, let me share a little bit about my personal journey, and how I arrived at where I am today.

I made my debut in the financial planning world selling life insurance in 1969. For thirteen years I worked as a branch manager at a large company in Ohio. Then I started wholesaling on Wall Street. My job was to go around to brokerage firms and educate them on various products. My specialty was life insurance and annuities, and I sold the heck out of those things.

Life insurance back then was different than it is today. In the old days, they had a product called single premium life that offered a death benefit just slightly greater than the premium and grew at 8-9%. Policy holders could take money out at 5%, but the company would credit that loan at 5%. In other words, it was a "wash loan"—a tax-free withdrawal from the account. The product was advertised in the *Wall Street Journal* and as you might expect, it was hugely popular ... until Congress de-legislated it in 1987.

By then I was working for Merrill Lynch as an inside wholesaler. I was an Estate Planning Specialist, helping stockbrokers in the Midwest out of Columbus, Ohio. If the brokers' clients were interested in estate planning or life insurance, the brokers would bring me in to help them figure out what products and techniques best met their needs.

I had been going to night school for my undergraduate degree, and once I graduated with a BA in Business Administration (majoring in marketing and insurance), I continued on to evening law school. I was working full time and going to law school at night. I like to say that my liver's in great shape, because I didn't have time to go drinking at the bar with my buddies! I attended night law school all year long, even during the summers, graduating and passing the Ohio bar in 1982.

In the mid nineties, I put my degree to use and practiced law as an estate planning attorney in Ohio, specializing in family wealth transfer and tax planning. It didn't take me long to realize that I liked being in the financial planning industry a lot better than being a lawyer. There's a great story about the attorney who dies and goes to heaven, and when he gets there, there's a long line. The guy's a famous attorney, and he's not used to waiting. So he pushes to the front of the line where Saint Peter stops him. "Everybody's treated equally here," St. Peter says. "Go back and have a seat."

The attorney turns around in a huff and sits back down.

A few minutes later, he sees a guy in a long white robe with a bunch of law books tucked under his arm. The guy walks right to the front of the line, says a few words to St. Peter, and gets ushered into heaven's pearly gates.

The attorney is livid. "Why'd *he* get to go in?" he yells.

"Well, sir," says St. Peter, "that was God. Every once in a while he likes to play attorney."

I love that story because I've found it to be so true. Many well educated professionals think they know everything about everything!

My law degree has certainly been helpful, but I knew that wasn't the field I ultimately wanted to be in. So I expanded my experience, working with brokers' clients in two of the nation's major national financial corporations. But there was an awful lot of bureaucratic red tape, and I spent more time in meetings than I did helping clients find financial solutions.

One day, an attorney friend called me up on the phone.

"Hey Bob," he said. "I know a guy doing seminars down in Florida. He's selling high-end life insurance and helping high net worth clients in Naples, Florida. You interested?"

You bet I was!

I moved to Florida and started my business above my garage. That first year, we were able to protect $3 million of our clients' retirement dollars. By last year, that number had skyrocketed to $44 million in one year. This year we are on pace to protect over 70 million dollars of our clients' money.

Today Grace Advisory Group: Tax and Retirement Specialists is in the top quarter of 1% when it comes to providing safe, tax-efficient retirement plans to grateful clients. We've got twenty-four employees and seven offices up and down the west coast of Florida, including our main office in Fort Myers, serving Naples, Bonita Springs, Cape Coral, Port Charlotte, Punta Gorda, Tampa, Sarasota, Sun City Center and The Villages.

In 2008, 2009, 2010, 2011 and 2012 *Fort Myers News-Press* readers named Grace Advisory Group: Tax and Retirement Specialists "Best Income & Retirement Planners." In 2009, 2010, 2011 and 2012 I was recognized by *Gulfshore Life* as a "FIVE STAR Wealth Manager: Best in Client Satisfaction," a distinction based not on sales volume but on how consumers evaluated their experiences working with our firm. I also host the radio show "Retire with Grace" every weekend, which airs on radio stations throughout Southwest Florida.

I got into radio because I felt it was a good way to get my message to retirees. This part of Florida is home to a large number of retirees—probably 40-60% are snowbirds who stay up north in the summer and come down here in winter. We tailor our workshops and seminars to these men and women, and I personally do around fifty of them a year. We hold them at nice restaurants like Ruth's Chris and Shula's, and we always get a great response. People are hungry for information about how to protect their retirement funds, reduce their taxes, increase their income and reduce their fees, especially in this sour economy.

Grace also does tax returns—between 1,600 and 2,000 a year. Looking at a tax return is like looking at the financial heartbeat of an individual. In fifteen minutes, I can look at your return and show you what would happen if you repositioned your money into financial instruments that offer written guarantees and tax advantages by removing dividends, interest, and capital gains from current taxation. The tax return is a great starting place, a quick way for me to show potential clients the many options available to them for safeguarding their money and reducing their taxes.

Radio shows. Seminars and workshops. Life insurance and tax returns. We even have an in-house attorney in Fort Myers to help our clients with their wills and trusts. At Grace Advisory Group: Tax and Retirement Specialists, we offer one-stop retirement planning. We pride ourselves on taking the complexity out of the process, making it as easy and pain-free as possible. Our mission statement is ***"To design and implement a financial plan that provides***

safety and the highest and most tax-favored income stream that cannot be outlived."

When a new client comes to me, gives me $100,000, and asks me to manage it, I'm going to ask a lot of questions like the following:

- "What do you want to accomplish with this money?"
- "How much liquidity do you want?"
- " What is this money for?"
- "Who is this money for?"
- "How much of your money do you want to protect?"
- "If this is your retirement money, how much can you afford to lose?"
- "Who helps you make your financial decisions?"

Before you jump into any kind of investment, it is important to think about how your life is going to be affected if you were to lose the money you invested. When you are answering my questions, if you are telling me that it's okay for me to take your money, invest it, and then lose it, then you are telling me that you are a gambler. And I have no desire to be your bookie!

People who are considered gamblers in the sense I just described are not interested in the 6-8% guaranteed conservative gains per year that I give my clients. My numbers are not exciting to them; my numbers aren't something for gamblers to brag about at a cocktail party. They want to hear me say, "I'm really good. My minimum gain for a portfolio is 12 to 15% a year. I know inside stuff about the tech industry or any industry you can name." If I talked this way, I would be sprouting words from a big bag of hot air—just like most "investment professionals" out there who continue to peddle risk. Warren Buffett himself said, "Give me a million dollars and a 'hot tip' and I'll lose it for you in a year."

The truth is that no one in financial services has complete information to make constant gains of 12 to 15%. Even Bernie Madoff only promised 10 to 15% gains! The reason brokers can't live up to their pie-in-the-sky promises is that they are salesmen who do not know, understand, or control the information that develops behind their backs. They are at the bottom end of the Wall Street food chain and only play the role of fee-only money managers to the firm's clients.

Furthermore, in the recent real estate bubble, lending institutions like Lending Tree, DiTech, WaMu, World Savings, and Countrywide were not going to tell their salesmen/brokers to slow down the volume of mortgages they churned out, even though the executives and salesmen on Wall Street knew that questionable loan underwriting was causing a dangerous, over-heated real estate market—the effects of which nearly threw the global economy into an unprecedented catastrophe.

If there's one thing I've learned over the years, it's that knowledge is control. I like to divide knowledge into three categories. Statistically, each of us knows about 20% of all the knowledge in the world. That means that "What we know" makes up a mere 20%! Your 20% is different than mine or anybody else's.

"What we know we don't know" is another 5%—the gaps in knowledge that we're willing to admit. I don't know calculus; I don't know how to speak Chinese or Russian or many other things.

But a whopping 75% falls under "what we don't know we don't know." And that's the part that can hurt you in a big way. In order to learn, you have to be willing to be open-minded and willing to listen to new ideas and concepts that you've never heard about before. As the historian Daniel J. Boorstin said, "The greatest obstacle to discovery is not ignorance—it is the illusion of knowledge."

So here's the question: How do we come up with a system that allows us to have guaranteed lifetime income that never runs out? How do we maintain that income so that our lifestyle does not diminish during retirement, but at the very least stays the same and hopefully improves, even in the face of rising inflation?

I'll tell you one thing: the answer isn't on Wall Street. Those guys have been selling the American people a bill of goods for the last forty years. They told trusting investors, "Give us your money and we'll make you rich." What happened for a lot of people was the opposite: the greed of the casinos made them poor.

And yet, people keep running back to Wall Street. It's like a young child who keeps running back to his abusive parent—they don't know where else to go. When it comes to your retirement fund, I call it "financial insanity": doing the same thing with your money that you've been doing for years, and expecting a different result.

As you read this book, I want to encourage you to keep an open mind. If you've been enticed by the opportunities Wall Street promised you, don't worry—you're not alone. What I want to show you is how an entirely different attitude, bolstered by different investment products and processes, will go a long way in protecting your money and your future.

I didn't discover these instruments and processes overnight. I've spent the last forty-three years learning about them, testing them, approving the ones that work, and throwing out the ones that don't. My clients are grateful for the breadth of my knowledge and experience, and I'm happy to help them keep their money and their lives intact.

The key point to remember is that retirement planning is significantly different than paycheck planning. We're no longer in the accumulation phase. It's time to move into the territories of preservation and distribution.

So how do you move into these later phases? Through something we call a Sequential Income Portfolio System, or SIPS. The concept on which SIPS is based is that short-term money—money you need right away—has the lowest rate of return. A one-year CD pays less than a five-year CD, five years pays less than ten years, ten years pays less than thirty, and so on. It's a simple principle: the longer the financial institution keeps your money, the longer time they earn more spread, hence the greater the return both to them and therefore to you.

But most of our clients cannot wait five to ten years for income. These men and women are, on average, sixty-five to seventy-five years old. They're past the paycheck phase, and they need immediate income.

Let's say Ken and Robin, a married couple in Naples, have $100,000. We take a *portion* of that money and put it into a five-year immediate annuity. Ken and Robin write a check to the insurance company, and thirty days later (after the paperwork is filed and approved), the insurance company starts sending them checks.

For the next five years, Ken and Robin get monthly checks of $500. That's $6,000 a year—6% of $100,000.

But that's only the first portfolio. SIPS allows us to put a mathematically determined portion of Ken and Robin's retirement money into a *second, third, and fourth* portfolio, maximizing the rate of return in each successive portfolio. At the end of the first five years, the first portfolio is empty. All the money in portfolio #1 has been paid to Ken and Robin. But now we turn our attention to the second portfolio, which has been growing for five years at a contractually guaranteed rate of return.

The second portfolio is now equal to the amount initially put into the first portfolio and will continue the $500 per month distribution to Ken and Robin for the second five years.

The third five years we're looking at a deferred fixed annuity, except this one is linked to an index, which gives you a portion of the growth of the stock market with none of the risk. With a fixed indexed annuity, if the market goes up, you're along for the ride. If it goes down, you don't lose a dime. It's not about what you make; it's about what you don't lose. Nobody, that I am aware of, has ever lost a penny of their deposits from a fixed legal reserve instrument, even during the 1929 depression. That's saying something!

At the end of the tenth year, the third portfolio is expected to have been grown to a value allowing a third five-year payout of $500 per month. The fourth portfolio, which has an income rider and has been growing for fifteen years at a guaranteed rate, will have regrown a guaranteed lifetime income account equal to $100,000, which will continue the $500 per month income to Ken and Robin for the rest of both of their lives. If they pass at a normal life expectancy, some or all of the $100,000 will be left for their heirs. Even if they live way beyond their life expectancy, their income will continue.

Simply put, SIPS means we're growing that money over the longer term while still ensuring a higher income in the short term. The money is spread over different portfolios or "legs," ensuring that, no matter what happens, Ken and Robin's retirement income will never dry up.

The fourth portfolio is actually a pension type account, with a guaranteed compound interest. When I tell people I can give them a guaranteed compound 6-8% and a 6-8% bonus on their money up front, they literally don't believe it. It's one of the biggest problems we face at the Grace Advisory Group: Tax and Retirement Specialists: making our clients understand that it's not too good to be true!

What does that mean for you? Say you've got $100,000 in your pension. That bonus means the insurance company adds $6,000-$8,000 to your account. You can't pick it up five years from now and go buy a car, but it will give you a guaranteed income no matter how long you live. Your pension account growth is guaranteed at a compound growth rate of 6-8%. You've got the bonus, so divide the bonus by ten years plus the guarantee rate and you have a guaranteed 6.7% to 8.8% compound growth over a ten-year period.

Here's the magic bullet: if the money used for the Sequential Income Portfolio System (SIPS) lifetime income program is "non-qualified money" (you've already been taxed on it), there will be huge tax savings on the income stream—as much as 97% percent tax-free the first five years, 78% tax-free the second five years, and 58% tax-free the third five years.

Why? Because of a little-known provision in the IRS tax code called the exclusion ratio applied only to "annuitized" withdrawals from non-qualified accounts. If you take your 10% withdrawals from an annuity, it's treated on a LIFO (Last In First Out) tax basis. Awareness of this little-known tax provision is one of the many benefits Grace Advisory Group: Tax and Retirement Specialists brings to our clients' table.

There's nothing else out there today that's fueling that kind of return. Bonds are 2-3%, banks are crawling along at ½%. I'm talking about a guaranteed 5-6% cash flow on your money that is generated from an account that is guaranteed to grow at 6.7% to 8.8% until the income stream begins—a heck of a lot better than the alternatives!

Among the depositories of retirement funds is one of the primary retirement assets of the last twenty-five years: the 401(k). The problem is that as much as your employer (and your broker) wanted you to buy into the 401(k) concept, it just flat out didn't work. As an investment "vehicle," for all too many people, it's standing broken down by the side of the road, a smoking pile of junk. So how did you—and so many others—become convinced that the 401(k) was the way to go? Why did Wall Street and your employer team up to offer you this failed approach to retirement investing? And what can you do right now if you did have a 401(k) (or a 403(b) for government employees) that has lost much of its value?

We'll turn to this critically important topic in Chapter 3.

chapter three

Why Qualified Retirement Accounts Never Let You Retire

Remember Fred from Chapter 1? He has a 401(k) retirement account, put money into it every single month, and did exactly what the big boys on Wall Street told him to do. So why can't he ever retire comfortably?

Let's take a deeper look at 401(k) and other retirement plans that are funded with risk investments and find out why they make money for everybody involved with the plan … except the poor schnook who's putting his hard-earned money in. Amazingly, Fred thought he was contributing to his own retirement. Instead, for the last twenty years, he contributed to comfortable retirements for a whole lot of people in the financial services industry.

Fred worked his whole career for XYZ Corporation. When 401(k) plans came in, Fred enrolled because all the "smart people" whose books he read told him to do so. Some people he knew just kept their money in the bank. "How boring," Fred thought, "They'll never have the money they need later on." Now it turns out that the boring people have more money than Fred. How could that have happened?

Every month for twenty years, through his 401(k) plan, Fred invested a portion of his income in stocks, bonds, or mutual funds, hoping that later on he could retire on the money he made on those investments. What Fred didn't know was that he was playing musical chairs with Wall Street. And he was losing the game from the day he started playing. The Wall Street executives, fund managers, and financial advisors were the players along with Fred. When the music stopped, they all got seats—because they knew when the music would stop. Poor Fred! Nobody ever took a moment to tell *him* when that moment would come.

From the mid-1980s to the present, Wall Street invited Fred and millions of other Americans to a game when billions of 401(k) dollars were put into the stock market ... and the real estate market. Wall Street executives should have known better. They should have known that mortgage-backed securities, which boosted the real estate market from 1999 to 2007, were potentially toxic in a real estate downturn (that is, the down cycles that have happened every ten to twelve years since 1945!). They likely saw the collapse of the real estate bubble coming. But they didn't say a thing to Fred about the risk that the mortgage-backed securities would have on the US and international stock markets and Wall Street firms. Instead, his broker encouraged him to invest in stocks and mutual funds. Now, most of Fred's money is gone.

What's the cost? Fred's 401(k) plan now won't let him retire on time or with the same amount of resources to support the lifestyle he desired. Fred wasn't expecting to retire to the south of France and live in a castle overlooking the beach. He thought he'd be able to stay in his house, pay for his and his wife Janet's expenses after she quits teaching, play some golf, and maybe get a motor home to visit the grandchildren. But poor Fred can't afford to quit working now that his 401(k) has dropped by 40%.

What's the cause for Fred's financial mess? There are actually two basic reasons: 1) the replacement of his company's core retirement program with the 401(k) plan and 2) the greed of Wall Street that drove the economy into the real estate and tech bubbles and other financial meltdowns. Let's take a look and see how these things played out.

A History of Financial Flubs

From about 1940 to the mid-1980s, people working in the private sector secured their retirement through their company's core pension program. The core program was usually modeled similar to the government's *defined benefits* program, which stated that if you worked X amount of years, you would get Y amount of money as a pension in each year of your retirement. The defined benefits program was the deal that federal and state employees like teachers, policemen, and firemen received.

In the private sector, for employers like XYZ Corporation where Fred worked, it was the company's responsibility to fund and manage the core retirement programs and ensure that these were part of the corporation's assets. The federal government was only a retirement guarantor of last resort if the private company experienced bankruptcy, defaulted, or faced other major financial challenges or setbacks.

The government's bailout of Chrysler back in 1981 was an interesting example of this arrangement. Congress gave $1 billion in loan guarantees to Chrysler to revive its operations when the company was on its last legs.

Congress opted to go that route rather than the more costly route of fulfilling its obligation to payout $1.5 billion for the company's pension plan in case of bankruptcy. But the Chrysler situation was very rare. Until then, most employers funded their pension plans appropriately and paid their retirees what they were owed.

The 401(k) plan was the more prominent supplemental program enacted by Congress. There was also the 403(b) plan for those people who worked for public education, churches, and non-profit organizations. Interestingly enough, from the introduction of 403(b) plans in 1963 to 1993, educators could only put annuities into their 403(b) plans. The Kennedy Administration mandated only safe, guaranteed investments for their plans. That changed in 1993 when Congress opened up the 403(b) plans to mutual funds in addition to annuities with the same disastrous results for those who shifted from safety to risk.

These supplemental programs (IRAs, 401(k), 403(b), 457, etc.) were also called *defined contribution programs*: The Internal Revenue Service (IRS) defined how much you were able to put into those plans in addition to what was put into the core program of your company. The supplemental programs were great programs because they enabled workers to retire and still receive darn near the same amount of money they had received in salary.

Even if you didn't have money to put into the supplemental programs, you still had your core program, and you learned to live with what you got. Even when people lost money in the supplemental programs for whatever reason, they would still have a back-up core program. A back-up plan is always good! So what happened? Why did those lucky workers with a pension do so well … and why did Fred do so poorly?

The key concept is that the corporate 401(k) plan and 403(b) plans for educators and government workers were ***never intended to be primary retirement plans***! They were intended to be ***supplemental***—to add to what your employer gave you in the core pension plan.

Then things changed. In the early 1980s, Congress, the accounting industry, the Wall Street lobbyists, the mutual fund lobby, and the 401(k) plan administrator lobby got together and decided that it was too hard for corporations to fund core retirement programs. Their reasoning probably included the following points:

1) Why use the resources of the corporation to manage a retirement program when workers can do it themselves?

2) We need somebody to buy the common stocks of the companies for which we underwrite; why not have millions of corporate workers become the buyers?

They concluded that corporate workers should have a 401(k) plan where they would put a portion of their incomes in Wall Street investments that are supposed to grow to fund their retirement instead of a company's core retirement plan. So the 401(k) plan went from being a supplemental plan to becoming *the primary retirement* vehicle for millions of American workers. Corporations only had to partially match the worker's contributions—that is, if the worker could even afford to contribute. The companies then forced the employee to remain with the company 3, 5, or 10 years in order to be eligible to be vested in that employer match.

Through the urging of different highly compensated Wall Street and 401(k) lobbyists, private sector companies like Ford, Chrysler, and several of the largest domestic airlines decided to be rid of their core retirement programs and set up 401(k) plans for their workers. Over the next twenty-five years, more and more companies eliminated their core retirement programs while the state, county, and city governments retained them for their employees. Currently, fewer than 30% of American companies still have core retirement programs. The responsibility of funding retirement has slowly been shifting and placed on the backs of private sector workers—people like Fred.

Workers were sold on the 401(k) idea originally because we were told that we would have more control over our retirement money. The 401(k) salesmen told us, "Wouldn't it be better to control your own retirement account? You could put money in stocks, bonds, or mutual funds, and probably do better than whatever your company's core retirement plan offers. You can tailor your own plan to your own risk tolerance. Think of it! You can be in control of your own destiny! Of course, we'll charge a fee or two for all that ... but still! You'll be the boss!"

How much control did workers really have? Did they have control over the fact that they lost money in stocks, bonds, and mutual funds in the 1987 stock market crash, during the recession of the early 1990s, during the tech bubble that burst around 2001, or during the recent economic meltdown? They had no control at any of those times!

In addition, how much control did workers really have over where they could invest their money through their 401(k) plans? They could only invest in stocks, bonds, and mutual funds that *paid commissions and fees to financial services firms and funds.* You couldn't stick your 401(k) money in any truly safe, risk-free investment like CDs or fixed insurance annuities. Why not? Because if you did, no one on Wall Street could make money off of you!

Would you like to put your 401(k) money in a bank CD? That's an investment guaranteed by the FDIC. Well, somehow, the 401(k) lobbyists and the rest of the Wall Street lobbyists excluded bank CDs from 401(k) plans. In fact, the lobbyists got Congress to say that we can't have products that have a *back-end surrender charge* (or a charge for pulling out funds before the completion of a certain period of time such as five years) on the menu for Fred's investments. Wouldn't you know it? CDs have back-end surrender charges! Fixed annuities have back-end surrender fees! What a coincidence! The lobbyists probably used this justification: "We were just trying to protect Americans from getting charged on their investments in case they changed their minds or needed their money for unforeseen emergencies."

Well, so much for protection! While Wall Street was convincing Congress to set down these favorable restrictions for 401(k) plans (favorable to Wall Street!) in the early 1980s, CDs and fixed annuities earned 12 to 14% annually without risk, while the stock markets were hovering at Depression-era levels (adjusted for inflation). Wall Street desperately needed to figure out a way to bail itself out of a depressed market. It succeeded with the newfound supply of funds to purchase stocks and mutual funds through the 401(k) plans of the American worker.

When a downturn happens, the Freds of the world ask, "Why are there no safe options in my retirement plan?" The harsh but simple answer is that Wall Street doesn't want Safe options like CDs and annuities because they won't make any money that way. If you can't use bank CDs and annuities for your 401(k) account, you are stuck with the tried and true casino games provided by Wall Street. With a fee here and a charge there, Wall Street firms stood to benefit enormously from 401(k) plans. And they did. They made millions and millions of dollars from charging your investment account, whether or not you made money.

So we see that the replacement of a company's core retirement plan was to Wall Street's financial benefit. They now receive money that was yours at one time; however, you bear all the risk—not your corporation (Wall Street's partner in crime is the company, who historically had to fund your retirement with conservative investments).

The Wall Street casino could take a devastating toll on 401(k) investments, even if the average Fred thinks that he played his cards right. Here is a rough summary of how the process works. A Wall Street firm goes to a company and says, "Hey, let us raise money for you by selling an interest in your company called a common stock." When a company agrees, the Wall Street firm has to sell the stock to somebody in order to raise funds for development and growth. Why not stick some stocks and mutual funds into Fred's 401(k) account as Fred contributes monthly to his plan under the direction of his plan's brokerage custodian? After all, Fred checked a box that indicated he had some tolerance for risk!

Just how much risk is Fred bearing? Well, if Fred buys the stock or shares of the mutual fund, he owns 100% of the risk of the stock if it loses value. And he doesn't even know he bought the stock because his fund managers bought the stock for him. So the risk of the company's stock is borne not by the sharks on Wall Street but by the minnows on Main Street.

Mutual fund companies have a huge desire to purchase common stocks with the money in people's 401(k) accounts under their management. The fund advisors will call their investors like Fred and ask if they would like to invest in a utility fund that contains stocks from AT&T or General Electric, tech funds, healthcare funds, or real estate funds. Wall Street is thrilled that mutual funds are doing billions of dollars of transactions in 401(k) accounts and taking not-too-informed orders from Fred.

Fred doesn't really know if he is investing in the right companies. He is just listening to the advice of his advisors—who could be the low-paid clerks at the brokerage firm handling millions of inquiries nationwide or Fred's buddies in the lunchroom. Fred looks at his menu of investments and says, "Well, why don't I put some money in the Dow Jones, the S&P, this healthcare fund and that tech fund ..." Fred picks those investments with the same confidence he has trying to pick horses at the track; does he choose based on the bookie's information or "tout" sheets, the color of the jockey's shirt, or the lucky number of the horse?

Before 1982, less than 5% of the US population owned stocks. Then 401(k) plans went from being supplemental to being the main retirement vehicle for millions of Americans. The biggest holders of stocks in this country are now the Freds of the world, the people who hold 401(k) and other retirement accounts. Today, state pension funds such as the Florida Retirement System (FRS) Pension Plan have $130 billion invested, and over 60% of the money is in stocks. (I was told by some actuaries of several state public employee pension funds, teachers' funds, and military funds that their funds need to make about 6 to 7% a year for a period of time in order to adequately fund everyone's retirement over time—40% drops are devastating to them and ultimately to taxpayers who must bail out those retirees!) Add to that the amount invested in the corporate stocks from other pension and mutual funds, and you witness an explosion in the stock market since the early '80s.

With the proliferation of 401(k) plans, stocks were sold at a higher volume, and they also had greater volatility—they could swing up or down more quickly with the emotional knee-jerk tendencies of the investing public. Before the explosion, the Dow Jones Industrial Average was at 800 in 1982. These numbers turn out to be lower than the Dow in the 1930s when adjusted for inflation. However, as 401(k) plans gained popularity from 1983 on, we saw the Dow Jones go as high as 14,000 by October 2007 and then back down to 6,500 just eighteen months later (a loss of 53%) as we all painfully witnessed in early 2009. At the time of this writing in early August 2011, we're coming out of the worst week for the S&P 500 and NASDAQ on an average basis since November 2008, and the worst week for the Dow since March 2009. In some ways, things have gotten better; in others, worse.

Fred's participation, along with the participation of millions of other average folks, generated huge demand for common stocks. From 1984 to 1987, stocks grew in price. The Dow went from 800 in 1982 to over 2600 in 1987. Wall Street was elated because its firms made 2.5% and 3% annually in fees off your money invested in retirement plans … whether you made money or not. And the mutual funds and brokerage firms make *25 to 30% of your account value over a ten-year period* from your money by peddling risk. Further subtract the bite of taxes on your gains, and you're lucky to be left with a 50% net of your imagined gains!

However, there's a reason why stocks are considered risky—there is always the chance that you will lose big. All of a sudden, in October 1987, the Dow dropped 33% in two weeks from 2600 to 1739. That was, to say the least, devastating!

Before that crisis, a lot of people who bought stocks borrowed against the rising value of their stocks to buy new houses or cars, take vacations, and invest in businesses. They might have borrowed up to 70 or 80% of the value of their stock portfolio. These people woke up one day and discovered their stocks were down about 30%. Then came many margin calls: Brokers demanded that these investors put more money in their portfolios or sell some assets to make up the loss. Many people got wiped out in late 1987 because of the added pressure of folks having to sell their stocks when they didn't have more cash to put into their accounts.

After that experience, people wanted to be more careful, so it took several years before the market returned to a bullish attitude. Then around the mid-90s, we saw a buying frenzy stoked by a Wall Street-created bubble in the tech industry. The bubble involved thousands of companies that had no sales, no revenues, and no earnings per share. Wall Street analysts made up stories about the viability of these companies. All of a sudden, you called your brokerage firm, whether it was Fidelity or Schwab or another large firm, and you asked, "What's up? What's hot?" And they would tell you about the tech stocks. You might then rush to get out of the secure blue-chip stocks and jump into the tech stocks, investing $100,000 or even over a million dollars because you didn't want to miss the boat! As always, it's your *fear* of missing the gains or having losses versus Wall Street's *greed* for making money whether you do or not—and all of it fueled by *worry* created by Wall Street's engine of misinformation.

From 2000 to 2003, the market went down almost 46% because it was obsessed with tech stocks that had absolutely no value. Probably 80% of tech companies involved in the bubble went out of business, and investors lost the majority of their investments. The 401(k) account holders got cleaned out of a boatload of money from 2000 to 2003. How could I even put people's anger into words? That would take another book!

From 2003 to 2007, the market finally got back to where it was in early 2000: It gained 60% off its 2002 lows. But we had a new bubble; this time it was called real estate. Once again Wall Street fueled the engine of *greed*. Real estate grew so dramatically during that time that Wall Street got together with the banks and created instruments called "Collateralized Debt Obligations" (CDOs). Wall Street said to the banks, "Hey, we've got a great deal for you. Put together as many loans as you can—hundreds of thousands of them. We'll break them up, package them, and sell them to pension funds, mutual funds, foreign governments, and the general public in their 401(k) plans. You make huge fees and bonuses—we make huge fees and bonuses—and guess who assumes all the risk for this new casino game?"

This CDO party went on for years, and things got so overheated that lending institutions loaned money to people who could not have qualified for a loan under normal, prudent underwriting standards. Mandated by the government, big loans were given to people who couldn't pay their small loans. But now, many of these people qualified for a loan for home purchases by just having a pulse! Nearly everyone qualified for a home loan from 2000 to 2007 as the lax underwriting of the greedy lenders didn't even check to see if they had jobs!

For example, at the insistence of Congress from 2002 to 2007 to help low-income families to partake in the explosion in real estate prices, loans were made available to people in low-income communities in Southern

California and other parts of the country who could not afford to repay those loans. It seems that nobody at any of the lending institutions involved in peddling the mortgage-backed CDOs did the basic prudent mortgage underwriting or reality checks to ensure that the people to whom they lent were able to qualify and repay the loans. Easy money always creates an over-bought environment—whether in stocks or real estate!

Wall Street likes to keep pushing stocks until the end of the line even after the firms made their fees, executives exercised their stock options, and the analysts received their bonuses. The real estate bubble fueled easy money, easy credit, and improper underwriting. Now banks like Countrywide, WaMu (now Chase), IndyMac, and Wachovia are bailed out for Wall Street's and the lender's greed after 401(k) holders lost 40 to 50% of their money in the stock market, while seeing their real estate values plunge 30 to 40% in just two short years. So the executives of the lending institutions and Wall Street got theirs—but what about Fred? You guessed it … he's left holding the bag, a bag which contains about 40% less money than it did a year ago!

Some firms were also pushed to the edge of sanity. Follow me closely on this one. The giant insurer AIG thought it was taking advantage of an opportunity and getting a piece of the CDO pie when it proposed to reinsure the market value of mortgage securities to the institutional investors who bought them. Wall Street responded, "Great! Now we have an exit strategy for an overheated market." Suddenly, when the real estate bubble burst and investors of CDOs lost money, AIG had to honor insurance contracts for the purchasers of the mortgage securities. But AIG couldn't honor all the contracts because even though it had assets, it didn't have time to sell off other assets to obtain the cash to pay its reinsurance obligations on those toxic mortgage pools. AIG formed a new game in the Wall Street casino, and it lost.

Before the bubble, the AIG life insurance and annuity divisions were (and continue to be) as solid as they can be. AIG made hundreds of millions of dollars in fees on insurance and annuity premiums. So it didn't need to play the CDO game, but it did so because of greed. The US government had little choice but to bail out AIG because the company was so big that its failure might have taken down the entire global economy. But where's Fred's bailout? Nowhere, of course!

After the real estate bubble had burst in mid-2007, there was a lot of finger pointing. The truth is the real estate bubble represented a new game of chance that formed in the Wall Street casino. Organizations such as AIG and WaMu participated in the game of chance, and everyone lost this time—not just Fred. But only Fred took a lasting hit, because the Federal Reserve was never going to bail out Fred. Instead, what was left of Fred's hard-earned cash (turned into tax dollars) was used to bail out the very institutions that had nearly destroyed the economy in the first place!

When 401(k) and Wall Street lobbyists convinced Congress and the Department of Labor during the 1980s that CDs and life insurance annuities (which guarantee principal during accumulation and a lifetime income) weren't a good idea for Fred's menu of investment options for his 401(k) plan, they were not looking out for Fred's interest. Now Fred calls his advisor, who is one of those good-old boys on Wall Street, and says, "I'm sixty-five years old. I can't afford to lose any more money. What options have you got for me?"

The only option that the advisor has for Fred is to put his money in bond funds, which are considered less risky than stock funds. But just how safe are bond funds? During the stock market debacle of 2008 and 2009, the average bond fund went down *15%.* It is absolutely criminal that Fred has no Safe options. Compared with stock funds, it was slightly less of a beating. But was it justifiable? No way!

Let's take another look back in history. As we discussed earlier, the stock market was so bad during the 1930s recession that it took about 25 years, until 1954, for the Dow Jones Industrial Average to get back to where it was in 1929. In fact, if you had put your money in a bank or other conservative investment that only gave you 4.7% per year, you would have matched the performance of the Dow from 1929 to 1973! Now, you might ask yourself, what's the point of trying to pick the best funds and the best stocks in the first place if all I needed along the way is just a 4.7% annual return on my investments? Good question. It sure isn't worth the lost sleep and ulcers!

From 1996 to 2003, only 24% of mutual fund managers outperformed the leading indexes—NASDAQ, S&P 500, and Dow Jones. Doesn't it make more sense to just put money in the indexes through no-load mutual funds and let them do what they do instead of spending all that time, money, and resources trying to find the next hot fund or market sector? Study after independent study proves that you will beat the professionals 76% of the time! Wouldn't your bookie like those odds?

After the last six years, 90% of professionals did not beat the indexes. In addition, even in desperate times, financial advisors were *still* not giving advice in their clients' best interest. In 2007 and 2008, financial advisors actually encouraged people to go into the Chinese and Indian stock markets when things started slowing down in the American market. But once people set foot into

Asian waters, they drowned, and their stocks went down 60% while our market went down 50%. It's almost like the financial advisors ensured that you didn't miss the opportunity to lose more money in the Chinese casino.

In a segment that aired in the spring of 2009, Steve Kroft from CBS's *60 Minutes* interviewed the leading 401(k) plan lobbyist to Congress and asked how they could allow these losses to happen. He smugly answered that the problem wasn't created by the 401(k) administration industry; the problem lies with the *investment community*. In other words, Wall Street!

The lobbyist also stated that people like Fred *should have known* that they were putting money at risk when they put money in their 401(k) mutual funds. With that answer, Steve Kroft's mouth dropped open. Where was the conscience in that answer? How do the financial wizards of Wall Street sleep at night, disavowing any responsibility for having destroyed the retirement dreams of the millions of investors who trusted them?

The bottom line is that even though the stock market has begun to rise again after this devastating loss of wealth, don't get too excited. You are still charged fees. Your money is still at risk. Chances are that *the market will never go up enough to recoup the losses you suffered in the past—especially if you don't have a lock-in mechanism to handle the possibility of future downturns.* If you are close to or in retirement you probably don't have enough of that oh so important ingredient—time. In addition, Wall Street will most certainly come up with another market-frenzied bubble, maybe this time in commodities like oil or metals that certainly should go up because of the devaluation of our currency after the extreme increase of the money supply by the Fed to prevent a global meltdown. Wall Street will regenerate the public's appetite for risk and entice Congress to stay the course with the present 401(k) plan structure instead of allowing the public to shift their 401(k) menu options to safe savings programs prior to age fifty-nine and a half.

We can only conclude that Wall Street and their 401(k) system is just one vicious shark frenzy tank. Millions of Freds are dropped into the tank but don't know why they are in the tank or how they got there. That's why you will never be able to retire with peace of mind from possible future catastrophic losses … as long as the current flawed investment system remains in place.

So if the 401(k) plan doesn't work, what will? What do you really need in order to create a retirement that Wall Street can't destroy? You need three things: *knowledge*, *understanding*, and *control* over your own retirement savings. You need to have the flexibility of being able to invest in Safe options not offered by your employer's 401(k) plan.

I'll now describe for you the Safe alternatives, so you can learn how to protect your money. And, Fred, if you're reading, I have good news. It's not too late to save your retirement dreams … if you take the advice you'll find in the next chapter.

chapter four

SIPS: The Power of Indexing

We now know that the 401(k) isn't a surefire ticket to retirement because it's fundamentally unsafe. But what *is* safe?

I was led to this philosophy through the revelation that *making money without incurring risk* is possible. In fact, it is just silly to play with risk when you don't have to or may be harmed by doing so.

The Idea Behind Indexing

So what's this system all about? What are the specifics of this approach to investing?

A lot of people hope that in the future, someone may be smart enough to create a financial product with the potential to only give investors gains and never losses. What Wall Street doesn't tell you, or is afraid to tell you, is that such a product already exists. My clients have been using it since 1998; it's called the "Fixed Index Annuity."

The fixed indexed annuity is basically a contract with an insurance company. The insurance company says to you, "Give us some money, and we'll guarantee that your principal investment will never be lost. And you will receive either a stated annual interest rate or participate with us in the growth of the stock market without risk of loss." They have been making and keeping that promise of principal protection to their clients for over 120 years.

Pretend that you gave the insurance guys $100 to invest this year in a fixed indexed annuity. They guarantee that you will not lose the $100, and you choose whether you want to receive the declared interest rate for one year (say, 4%) or to participate in the gains of a stock market index (like the Dow, S&P 500, or NASDAQ). The insurance guys, just like the bank guys, are in the business of making money on your money at no risk to them. If the stock index goes up 10% for the year, you would get about 70% of the gains, and they would pocket the difference. So your $100 investment would now have grown to

$107. You give up a percentage of the upside in order to eliminate 100% of the downside.

If the market is down, you don't make anything (nor do they), but you don't *lose* anything either. You then take your same account value and go on to the next year. The insurance companies accomplish this security by buying one-year options on that index. You are never in the market. The insurance uses its army of PhDs and super computers to accomplish this for you. If the markets gain, everyone wins. If the markets lose, the insurance company only loses the cost of the option. In either case, you don't lose any value from your account. This strategy is called *indexing*, and you will never lose money using it.

The beauty of *indexing* using the fixed indexed annuity is that your gains will be "locked-in" each year and shielded from the shocks and falls in the stock market. As I mentioned, your principal of $100 and the $7 you will make on it the next year comes to a total of $107. This $107 balance will be locked-in going forward, and you will not lose it, even though you might not make any more money the year after due to a downturn in the markets. Your principal *and the earnings on your principal* are guaranteed. I'm sure you can see the huge contrast between this lock-in feature in the fixed indexed annuity and the lack of this feature in mutual funds!

In 1963, when the Kennedy administration formulated the 403(b) plans for educators, the *only* investment option allowed for the 403(b) was a fixed annuity. Aside from US Treasuries, fixed annuities were considered the safest option in which to invest. Many people have clients who started their retirement accounts back in the '60s, and to this day, they haven't lost any money because of the fixed annuity products in their 403(b) plans. Even in the terrible market downturn of the 1980s, they made 12 to 15% a year and slept very well at night!

A variable annuity is a whole different ballgame. The insurance company gets a tidy fee to put you into a mutual fund (another tidy fee deducted from your money), and you are fully at risk for this extra, unnecessary layer of aggravation, illiquidity, and risk. Unlike a fixed annuity, a variable annuity can be thought of as a soup of risk-bearing ingredients—typically mutual funds that invest in stocks and bonds—all packaged (and therefore seemingly made legitimate) by the insurance companies.

In other words, insurance companies place their reputations for integrity and reliability on a product that offers neither the safety nor the guarantees of traditional fixed annuities. By contrast, the fixed indexed annuity was born out of the desire of the insurance companies to compete against Wall Street for management of retirement funds, not join the pigs at the trough. The competing edge for insurance companies is that they can guarantee your principal and the earnings on your principal, while Wall Street cannot. Insurance companies unwisely developed the variable annuity because they felt that they had to offer products with greater growth potential to compete with Wall Street in the '90s when the stock market was doing well. It has been a decision that by and large most insurance companies regretted when the stock markets collapsed from 2000 to 2002 and from 2008 to 2009. And it looks like we are looking at another challenging economy in the foreseeable future.

I hope you believe what I have to say about the benefits of fixed annuities, but it's always nice to have some real world backup. How about the Wharton School of Business? It's one of the most respected business schools in the world; the Wharton Financial Institutions Center completed a study in October 2009 entitled "Real World Index Annuity Returns." They wanted to determine just how beneficial annuities were for real people because most of the studies that had already been published were either pro-annuity (if they were paid for by the annuities industry) or anti-annuity (if they had been produced for the securities industry). No surprise there! Here's what the authors of the independent study determined:

The reality is at least some index annuities have produced returns that have been truly competitive with

Certificates of Deposit, fixed rate annuities, taxable bond funds, and even equities at times. … How will index annuities perform in the future? We do not know but the concept has proven to work in the past and any articles should reflect this. … The FIA is designed for safety of principal with returns linked to upside market performance.[1]

If I say it, you may or may not believe it. But now you've got Wharton saying the same thing, and I think you can count on their objective analysis.

Similar to the insurance companies' fixed annuity business, commercial banks also ensure that your deposits and the earnings on your deposits will not be lost. That explains why commercial banks and insurance companies are typically among the largest, strongest, and most secure financial institutions in the world. Now, I'm *not* talking about banks and insurance companies that jumped on the risk wagon and traveled past the speed limit, such as those involved with creating and packaging toxic mortgage-backed securities. Those greedy knuckleheads thought they could create excessive fees by loosening

---

1 Marrion, Jack, Vander Pal, Geoffrey, and Babbel, David F., Real World Index Annuity Returns, Wharton Financial Institutions Center, Personal Finance, October 5, 2009.

http://fic.wharton.upenn.edu/fic/cappolicy%20page/RealWorldReturns.pdf

their underwriting standards for real estate loans and then make additional fees by packaging and selling the toxic, over-valued mortgage pools to another set of knuckleheads called Wall Street. Now 80% of them are out of business—or would be, if our tax dollars hadn't bailed out their sorry backsides!

Take one more look at the difference between Wall Street firms and insurance companies. Wall Street makes money whether you do or not, and when the ship's going down, the captain is the first in the lifeboat called bailout money, while you never get to the lifeboat! Who bailed *you* out? Commercial banks and insurance companies typically make money with you—not in spite of you.

Suddenly, blue-chip firms like Merrill Lynch, Fidelity, and TD Ameritrade are touting retirement plans similar to the fixed annuity products offered by insurance companies for around a hundred years. They do so because they have to regain their reputation of being able to manage and grow retirement funds and not lose funds as they did in the recent decade-long downturn. What I have to say to them is this: How the heck are you going to regain your reputation after you have already lost half of your customer's money? You only want them to stay at risk in your casino in order to try to recover your losses. Likewise, casino blackjack dealers love it when you think you have to double down your bets in order to hit the big pot to make up for your earlier losses.

SIPS involves accumulating money in a safe way, never losing what you accumulated, and coming up with a plan that will pay you out for as long as you live because you don't want to outlive your money. In addition, it's learning to live the "Enough" lifestyle. For our clients, the fixed indexed annuity is doing a great job keeping their money safe with its lock-in mechanism for their annual returns and guaranteed annual payments during retirement. Their assets don't fluctuate wildly based on Wall Street's whims, and they are worry-free from the devastating stress and emotional damage that overtakes people who don't escape the gambling mentality. Our clients have control of their money, and the peace of mind to pursue the relationships and activities that they dreamed of during their working years.

Wall Street's Dirty Little Secret

If a fixed annuity is so great, then why aren't more people putting their money into it? The reason is the marketing and sales agenda of its opponents. Wall Street has always told you that you don't want annuities because insurance companies are charging large surrender fees. Surrender fees apply when you change your mind and want to take your money out of the annuity before the completion of the five- to ten-year period dictated by your contract. If there is an unforeseen emergency that requires you to take money out of your fixed annuity, things become inconvenient because you lose a percentage of your money. Now you know that's the string attached to a fixed annuity. But that's a lot better than living with all the risk! After all, everything has a string attached.

There are also scenarios where a fixed annuity is just outright dangerous. Imagine Charles, a seventy-five-year-old man in small town mid-America (where houses cost $80,000 to $250,000). He has only $50,000 to his name and nothing but Social Security to support him. (By the way, Social Security was created with the same mentality as 401(k) accounts—it was meant to be supplemental, not the primary source of retirement income.)

Now Charles wants someone to help him manage his $50,000. An advisor comes along and sells him a fixed annuity contract. Months later, Charles wants to take his money out of the annuity but only gets $45,000 back because of surrender fees. That is a criminal situation where the advisor was a salesman who didn't care for the well-being of his client. Still, at least the poor guy didn't lose all of his money when the stock market crashed in 1999—because he was in a fixed annuity. We see that even when an inappropriate fixed annuity recommendation occurs, it is still—in the bigger picture—better than a recommendation for a risky mutual fund.

I hope I'm clear that there are downsides to fixed annuities—no investment is perfect. But I want you to see that the surrender charge is just one negative compared to many positives. People buy a fixed annuity because they want three good things to happen: a lifetime income solution to pay for life's needs, *guaranteed* principal to insure that the income from the annual payouts doesn't run out too soon, and flexibility to take out 10% per year of the invested money if needed. To alleviate the inconvenience of surrender fees, I stress distributing the portion of your assets you need liquid into CDs and money market accounts, in addition to fixed annuities, so that you have other liquid sources of money.

If at some point down the road you need to pay surrender fees, you might be relieved to hear that the fees might just come from the growth value of the annuity. Of course, there is the chance that the fees dig into the principal; for example, you might be forced to pay 10% on a principal of $100,000 when your investment has only grown to $105,000. However, think about the people with 401(k)s who didn't put their money in fixed annuities and are losing many times the value of your surrender fees due to losses in stock value.

Moreover, the upfront and one-time commission that you pay the insurance companies to start a fixed annuity contract (although your account is credited with 100% of your deposit, unlike stock mutual funds) is amortized by the insurance company over the first few years. Many fixed annuities actually add a day one bonus to your account. Compare that with the 2.5 to 3% commission fee that you pay Wall Street *year after year after year.*

Ten years in a mutual fund or managed stock account means between 25 and 30% came off your account value whether you made money or not! I'm sure you'll agree with me that the potential risk of loss at the Wall Street casinos and the accompanying stress overshadows any commissions charged on a fixed annuity, particularly because they do not come out of your original investment. Solid advice that causes your accounts to gain without stress and grief over many years should be worth the commission that the insurance company (not you) pays me.

Another thing keeping people from getting into fixed annuities is the warning of some well-known financial advisors to never put an annuity in a tax-deferred qualified retirement account because the annuity growth is already tax deferred. A qualified retirement plan is a plan that meets certain requirements of the Internal Revenue Code and thus receives certain tax benefits like tax deferral. This means that the growth on your fixed annuity will not be taxed until you withdraw the money. (In contrast, you pay taxes on the growth of your CDs even though you never withdrew the money you put in the CDs.)

Some advisors would say that there is no use in putting a tax-deferred product in a tax-deferred account. Well, I say who cares what the tax status is as long as you are making money! Do you really care about the tax debate if the only other option is to lose big money with other, riskier options? Everything that comes out of a qualified retirement account is taxed anyway—just ensure that there's something left in there to be withdrawn! However, a variable annuity has fees deducted every year for the life of the contract while still being exposed to market losses.

You decide—a fixed annuity offering guarantees in your retirement account for no fee or a variable annuity in your retirement account with high annual fees and exposure to market losses.

The Truth about Bonds

You might be saying, "Okay, Bob. I get your point about fixed annuities. But what about bonds? Aren't bonds safe?" Great question!

I like to say that Wall Street is an "accumulation entity." In other words, Wall Street is in the business of *accumulating* assets. What Wall Street never figured out is this: Now that the money is there, what can be done to pay it out efficiently? In other words, they've never developed a lifetime income solution without any loss of principal for those who put their hard-earned dollars into risky investments. Wall Street's solution is usually bond funds because they typically pay periodic interest payments to its investors and are considered safer than stocks—that is, until the recent meltdown of the worldwide financial system threatened to bankrupt even the strongest corporations whose bonds are held in the trillions by mutual funds and pensions.

The problem with bond funds is that when interest rates rise, the value of your principal goes down. In that case, your principal is stuck in the bond fund and is prevented from growing in the high-interest-rate-induced market. As a result, there will be selling pressure on you to dump bonds and go into stocks or bond funds with greater risk and higher returns. But now your likelihood of losing money becomes greater. At the beginning of 2011, for example, the average long-term government bond had lost 9 percent.

A few brave souls might venture to ask their financial advisors if there are investment options that have a sort of lock-in mechanism that would prevent losses. The advisor might think of fixed annuities, US Treasury bond funds, or bank CDs but will never say a thing about them because the firm's executive team and analysts only care about touting stocks. The performance—and paycheck—of the typical investment advisor is based on the amount of stocks he sells or funds he places under management, not on how much safety and peace of mind he creates for his clients. The advisor would tell you to get into this stock or fund because the analysts tell the sales force and the public to do so.

Does this scenario sound familiar? It will strike a chord with many people who listened to such advice and lost tens of thousands. These losses should signal that it is time to leave the Wall Street casino.

Leaving their Wall Street brokerage houses to invest in a fixed annuity is not easy for many investors. Some people have developed tight relationships with their stockbrokers because these brokers have taken them out to lunch or dinner and sent them champagne at Christmas. As a result, they might feel obligated to stay with their brokers, not willing to make anyone feel bad or feel guilty for losing your money. But the truth is, all of us in the retirement planning business are salesmen, and it's our job to be personable people or else we won't succeed. Don't be fooled by sales pitches and proposals of friendship, and don't hesitate to say that you don't want your advisor's advice anymore. For God's sake, let them stay your friend, but quit enabling your "friend" to gamble with your life's savings.

I can tell you this—if my family doctor operated on my kids several times, and there were continual catastrophic results, I'd be sure to get a new doctor! Wouldn't you? Well, your financial advisor is your "money doctor," and their job is to make you healthy—not sick to your stomach!

Moreover, many investors fail to set boundaries about what they can or cannot afford to lose. These people are afraid to admit that they are not in control of their money because their brokers rule over it with an iron fist. Fearful of facing reality, some are not even looking at their statements and realizing that they are not getting the 10% annual returns on their investments as their broker had told them they would. After all the management fees, commissions, and taxes, what was said to be 10% might actually be 3-6% per year, or worse yet: significant losses. And remember you pay the freight even if you lose money!

The bottom line is that you need to examine closely the numbers that your advisor throws at you and make the decision that's best for you, not your advisor, about whether to stay with or leave your current brokerage house.

Does the SIPS Program Really Work?

Let's look at the following case study to understand how to apply the SIPS program if you have a 401(k) plan.

You probably don't know when you can retire. And you don't know what your options are while you are still working. Here's an interesting fact for you. In 2006, Congress enacted legislation that allowed people who are still working for their companies and still contributing to their 401(k) plans to transfer the bulk of their principal in their company's 401(k) to self-directed IRAs, where they are able to invest in products like a fixed annuity or another guaranteed savings vehicle. Employees can only do this if they are over fifty-nine and a half years old. The purpose of this legislation is to give people more control, flexibility, and choice concerning their investments but still allow them to continue to work with their employer. They can continue to contribute to their existing 401(k) even if they transfer money out of it to a self-directed IRA to lock-in and protect their investment portfolio.

This setup is called an *in-service distribution* because when you transfer your funds out, you can still be working for the company. Currently, about 70% of American corporations provide for an *in-service distribution*. Ask your company's 401(k) plan administrator if you are eligible to take advantage of this great tool to protect your retirement dreams.

Another important thing to know if you are *under* fifty-nine and a half years old is that if you have left your company and go to work for another, you can still move funds in the 401(k) plan of your old company to an IRA plan. If you left your 401(k) with the old company's 401(k) administrator, you are eligible to transfer it to an IRA, regardless of your age. Many people are not aware of this fact. That action is not an in-service distribution; it is considered a 401(k) rollover triggered by termination of employment. There are potentially millions of such rollovers eligible for transfer today, considering the countless job losses and job transfers.

Remember, an in-service distribution allows only those who are fifty-nine and a half years and over to participate. If you are "underage" (I bet nobody's called you *that* for a while!), then we would need to address the best options for you to get money out of exposure to risky markets within your current plan's menu choices. You may wish to go into a bond fund or money market fund where there may be less return but less risk by telling the 401(k) custodian to reduce your exposure to risk.

Grace Advisory Group: Tax and Retirement Specialists has always been able to give an accurate assessment of where somebody is going to be financially in ten, fifteen, or twenty years. Can Wall Street do that? Are you kidding me?! I think you know the answer to that one by now!

So how are we able to do that? Well, the financial products that we use have historically given us a predictable 6-8% annual return over the past twenty years. You probably realize that your money doubles every ten years at 7%. What has *your* portfolio done over the last ten years?

Let's say you're fifty years old, and you plan to retire at sixty-five. You have wisely come to me to ask me to manage your money. I can take out a simple handheld calculator and predict with pretty good accuracy what you will have in your retirement account fifteen years from now. I can calculate what you will accumulate based on guaranteed 6 to 8% compound growth of your retirement account and also project what your Social Security, real estate portfolio, and other pension plans will generate in income for you—and for how long.

You then give me $500,000 to put into a retirement account. Let me be modest and say that if I could get you a guaranteed 6 to 8% annual compound growth rate on that money, I would be able to double your money to $1,000,000 in just eight years—and quadruple it to $2,000,000 in sixteen years. At retirement, you could even take out 5 to 6% or $100,000+ each year, and this income stream will last you as long as you live. I can make all these calculations for you with no problem—with a $50 handheld HP calculator! Financial wisdom is not predicated on sophisticated, complicated technology. Numbers are your best friend, as long as the numbers aren't going down … and as long as they make sense to you!

This process that I just went through with you is so simple that it doesn't make sense to go to Wall Street for your retirement needs. Why stress yourself out in the Wall Street casino with its complicated risk games and unpredictability when my financial system can lay your financial future out in front of you clear and simple?

To put it even more simply, my approach follows the Golden Rule, which I will put this way: *Do for others what you wish to have done for you.* In this case, the rule means that when someone recommends a financial product to a client, he or she should think, "Would I recommend this product or strategy to my best friend or my mother?" If you are the client, don't be shy to ask the guy at the other side of the desk, "Would you put your mom in this?" Ask them if *their* life savings and retirement future are in this investment or strategy.

And my answer to that question? Yes. My wife and I have the majority of our life savings in these strategies as do my relatives and closest friends. Every single client of mine (over 1,200 clients) has their financial well-being tied to these strategies! None of our clients have *ever* lost one penny from our recommendations.

I've been in the retirement business long enough to promise you that the majority of Wall Street bookies do not own a large position in the stocks and funds that they recommend to you based on their firm's research. The reason is that they know the game, and they know the risk. They also know that Wall Street hits a down cycle every five to seven years, causing any stock that they recommend now to plummet—regardless of the fundamental touted by the research analysts—because when the public panics, everything goes down! And every bookie with over twenty years experience knows what it feels like to see the disappearance of his/her client base due to the confiscation of money by Wall Street's greed and shenanigans. More than likely, these stockbrokers themselves can't even afford to buy the same stocks that they recommend to others because they too have lost money in stocks or they've had their earnings reduced drastically when the casinos came crashing down. And they are advising you?

If you want the same retirement investment system that the person recommending it to you is using, then you should go with SIPS and other guaranteed strategies. And if you like casinos, stay away from Wall Street and go to Las Vegas. At least there, when you're losing your money, you can still catch a show and enjoy a buffet!

We know it's difficult to leave a long standing relationship with your current Wall Street advisor. But it's your money. Perhaps this Declaration of Financial Independence will make it easier for you.

Declaration of Financial Independence

Dear ______________________________ ,

Advisor Name

We appreciate all the work you have done for us over the years. However, at this time in our life we need to move to safety and guarantees. This is a family decision and is not open for discussion.

Regards,

____ ______________

Signature *Date*

chapter five

The Four Pillars of a Worry-Free Financial Plan

In this chapter, I want to share with you the foundation of the financial plan used by hundreds of my clients and highly recommended by other leading experts. It rests on four principals or pillars, so you can clearly see the strength of the system and why it can last forever. Taking the worry out of financial planning is one of my greatest gifts to my clients. I'm not performing magic. I'm just following the four-pillar investment approach, and I'd like to describe those pillars for you now. They are as follows:

1) Guarantee the safety of your principal;
2) Control and flexibility of your money;

3) A crediting method for growth on your money based on participation in the stock market gains, but not the losses; and
4) A lock-in mechanism that secures the growth of your account value to prevent losses during a future downturn.

Let's see how each of these will have a highly positive effect on your financial life.

The First Pillar: Guarantee

In today's world, most people think of the idea of **guaranteed principal** as wishful thinking. What do you mean "guaranteed principal?" Get out of town! It's impossible! The idea is almost bizarre to people who have lost large amounts of their principal in the stock market. So it takes a while for me to convince some of these individuals that it *is* possible to have a lucrative investment in which their principal is completely protected and completely guaranteed.

People were led to believe by Wall Street that in order to have a proper or aggressive return on their investment, they must be involved in some risk. In fact, society now correlates risk directly with return: More risk equals more return. If someone doesn't want to bear risk, he is considered the social outcast—the bench-sitter. He's ostracized socially. All his friends at the club brag about the risky nature of their investments because somehow that translates in their minds into being bold, swaggering, and success-oriented. Can you hear Wall Street asking you, "What's the matter, not tough enough?"

Of course, it never occurs to people that the "risk" part of the risk/reward equation might actually happen to them and that they will lose some or most of their hard-earned money. But they sure have in the last few years. Now they aren't bragging about risk anymore!

So, now that risk is a little less desirable, what types of investments exist that guarantee the safety of the principal? Investors who choose to avoid risk have limited options on Wall Street. They can either invest in CDs or bonds—products which don't yield much return. Consequently, less return means less money to retire on. If that happens to you, then you should be afraid, very afraid. By investing in CDs or bonds, you're really guaranteeing yourself losses—because the meager rate of return on those investments will never keep pace with inflation. That's especially true in light of the greater inflation rates we can all expect in years to come.

Wall Street knows that deep down, many investors are gamblers and actually *crave* risk. They prey on our fears that we won't have enough and that safe investments are all doomed to failure. (At least, the safe investments *they* offer are doomed!) So their ads, which appear to focus on offering you a great retirement through their investment products, are really intended to induce fear. If Wall Street succeeds in inducing fear in you, then they succeeded in their marketing and sales campaign to get you to invest in risky securities with them.

The big investment companies want clients to fear that they aren't making enough money so they have to invest with more risk, or that they will lose money if they don't invest and thus miss a golden opportunity. I don't call watching the Dow sliced in half in a matter of months a golden opportunity for investors, but they don't worry about your returns as long as you place your money under their control. Instead, they want you to fret that the train is leaving the station; you are either on it too late or too soon. If you are on it too soon, you should have waited for more risk to come along before getting on board with your investments. If you are on it too late, you watch everyone else make money while you are left behind. Either way, Wall Street wins by getting your money. The bottom line is that Wall Street has to continually inject worry into the mindset of the public.

You don't have to be stupid to fall for it. One of my clients is a successful cardiologist. At forty-seven, he's younger than my average client, and he's a very hard worker—he puts in ten to twelve hours a day in private practice. The guy is brilliant. He put a chunk of money ($75,000) in partnership in waterfront land in Florida. It took him less than six months to lose the whole nine yards. Why'd he jump in? Because his doctor buddies said, "What, you chicken?" and he didn't want to be left behind.

Contrast that with BC and RC, two of my favorite clients, who are both in their seventies and have taken their at risk Wall Street money and given me over a million dollars to protect. Through a wise and judicious blend of financial instruments and strategies, BC and RC have increased the value of their retirement account by hundreds of thousands of dollars over the last few years.

Another great client of ours is SV (a single lady) who has more than doubled her accounts in just over seven years with no market risk.

Every time you jump into the risk wagon with Wall Street, it's going to dump a lot of "wastepaper securities" on you. I define wastepaper securities as "the investments that knowledgeable investors are too smart to fall for." With this trend of "you jumpin' and them dumpin'," it is not a surprise that the principal you put into your investments is almost guaranteed ... to deteriorate if not evaporate altogether. When deterioration happens, people begin to lose hope of ever finding financial products that would guarantee the safety of their principal.

Now is the time that we pick ourselves up from the ashes and look for financial products that satisfy our first requirement of guaranteed principal. We covered the first steps in the previous chapters: doing your history homework to see what kinds of returns are *realistic*; finding the financial products that could get you those returns; and most importantly, protecting your principal investment. In addition, we have to understand what kinds of cycles and bubbles exist on Wall Street that would backfire on the investments we make and what kinds of products could be immune from those dangers.

Guaranteed principal is a must-have necessity to ensure that you have enough money with which to retire. You contribute to your retirement funds year after year and delay gratification so that you can enjoy life later. You shouldn't let Wall Street make your efforts worthless.

As we've seen, the one investment that definitely guarantees your principal is a fixed indexed annuity. My clients have never experienced a loss of their principal with this approach. Their principal is guaranteed by the financial strength of some of the largest, most stable insurance companies in the world, such as Allianz Life, ING, Forethought, Aviva, North American Life, Security Benefit Life, and American Equity.

Over the last 120 years, no policyholder of a legal reserve life or annuity contract has lost one dime of their original principal from their savings plans with these companies. They are rated by AM Best, Standard & Poor's, and Moody based on the quality of their investment portfolio (which is primarily investment grade bonds and government securities and some high grade mortgages) and by how much surplus over potential claims they have.

How much surplus do you think your bank has? Zero, and that's why they need the FDIC to cover any liquidity problems when there's a run on the bank!

The guarantees for my clients are not only on the original savings principal but also on the future account values that have grown from interest crediting. During the negative years in the stock market, my clients make and lose nothing, but during the positive years, they make about 70% of the gains made on Wall Street. Their gains are also locked-in along with their principal to prevent losses down the road as they approach retirement so that their lifetime incomes will not be diminished. We will discuss the importance of this lock-in mechanism later on.

The Second Pillar: Control and Flexibility

Now let's turn to the second core pillar: **the issue of control and flexibility.** Having control and flexibility over your retirement planning isn't just about having a 401(k) plan but also about controlling your real estate portfolio and your other savings programs. In addition, you also control "nonqualified" assets such as money obtained from inheritances or properties you may have sold. Even though these assets are nonqualified because they are not directly in your retirement fund, they are still part of the stash of cash from which you will live in the future.

Every asset you accumulate over the course of your lifetime should be viewed as continually flowing into a large pot of money from which you will draw your retirement paycheck. The ultimate goal of all our investments is to have a pot of money down the road that provides more income than our budget requires.

I always define "wealth" as having more money coming in from savings and investments when you retire than what's going out to pay your lifestyle necessities—without having to work or receive Social Security or other assistance from family! The shame is that only 5% of Americans fall into this definition.

We have a lot of different things in our pot of money that we need to control and manage. Nowadays, 60% of that needed pot of money is no longer located in our employers' core retirement plans since, as we've seen, most of the core plans have been replaced by 401(k)s. As a result, our control and flexibility over our retirement money is reduced because 401(k)s are managed by somebody else. And that "somebody" is the Wall Street casinos. Since you've read this far, you know that can't be good for you!

Let's take a quick moment to describe what I mean by control and flexibility over your savings and investments. Control is the ability to liquidate or refinance the asset WHEN you need it—not when or at the dictates of the market or economy! In other words, you have no control (and therefore no flexibility) over your savings or net worth if you don't know what the account or asset will be worth at a future time when needed or if you are unable to make a phone call and receive the funds in a timely manner.

If your money is "buried in your backyard" as real estate equity and you need cash fast for emergencies or income needs, you have to ask your banker for YOUR money—and then hope the economic climate isn't like the situation in 2008 or 2009 when you do so. Nothing is more upsetting than witnessing someone who was diligent in paying off all or most of their home who needs cash to pay bills when they lose a job, get disabled, or become sick and the lender says "Yeah, I know the money's buried in the backyard, but you can't qualify to pay it back!"

Also, good luck getting a sell order into your broker to get out of the stock market when it's in a freefall during a panic. The government can shut down the stock markets for a week to cool things down, and who knows what your stocks will be worth after it reopens.

Another vital aspect of controlling your money is this: *Never invest in a limited partnership or any passive investment that limits your access to the money when you might need it or want out for a better opportunity.* You may be giving money to people who may be unable to run a successful business venture or who have no control over economic variables like housing or energy recessions, high inflation, terrorism, or natural disasters. But they sure can give a good sales pitch about why you should invest with them and trust their ability to make you as much money as they'll make upfront off you.

Moreover, when the company run by the general partners fails, you won't be able to get your money out because, as limited partner, you do not have liquidity or a say in the financial decisions that affect your money. For example, some real estate and oil and gas limited partnerships in the mid-1980s and early 1990s failed and drained their investors' money. And these were put together by huge Wall Street entities! The limited partners could do nothing but wait for the destruction to settle and see if there was anything left after the class action suits were filed. They received pennies on their hard-earned dollars. These investors weren't stupid people. They were doctors and lawyers and other professionals … who got taken for a ride on Wall Street.

The lesson I've sought to impart throughout this book is ***never relinquish control of your finances to other people.*** When you allow someone else to be in charge of your money, someone like a broker at a major Wall Street firm, you abdicate responsibility for your own future well-being. You need to call the shots on not only your 401(k) plan's investment decisions but also all your other assets because everything you have contributes to your retirement pot.

Remember that if you cannot make a call and receive your money in a timely manner when you need it, you have no control. If you are unable to tap the cash buried in your "backyard" or your rental properties for emergencies, you are not in control of your money—the bank is!

The Third Pillar: Long-term Low Risk

Now let's examine the third pillar: **participation in long-term stock market performance without stock market risk.**

Historically, the stock market will give us 8 to 10% annual returns over a period of fifteen to twenty years, not the 20 to 30% that the blue-chip firms are advertising.

Moreover, we don't know which periods of time will give us only 5% and which periods will give us 10%. We don't know when the next big storm will be that could wipe all our investments clean. These storms (defined as at least 30% declines) happened in 1972-1975, 1981-1984, the early '90s, 2000-2002, and recently in 2008-2009. Anyone with a lick of business common sense knows that cyclical storms interrupt periods of sustained growth in stocks or real estate, but no one can predict exactly when they will occur. No one but the Fed and the Wall Street bankers knows when the credit markets will dry up yet again, causing the "musical chair panic" called recession.

If we look more closely at the returns that investors received over the last decade or so, we will see that most are no better off than they were in 1996. Let's take a look at Cindy, who put some money into the stock market in 1996. She made 85% on her money from 1997 to 2000. Then she lost it all—the growth and some of her principal with the 46% market decline during the tech bubble from 2000-2002.

Wait a minute! How does a 46% loss wipe out 85% gain? Well, Cindy's $100,000 in 1996 grew to $185,000 by early 2000. Then the 46% loss reduced her account value to $100,000—back to square one, if you will. Remember when I told you that stock losses hurt you more than gains help you?

She regained most of what she lost during 2003-2007 when the markets gained 65%, taking her account back to $165,000. Recently, though, in 2008-2009, Cindy lost 25% as the overbought real estate and stock market bubble burst. In 2011, she lost an additional 10% as the economy continued to flounder. Now, not only has she lost all her gains, but this latest loss took her all the way back to her 1996 account value of around $100,000! It has been a lost fifteen years for Cindy.

Had she used an indexed annuity with a lifetime benefit income rider guaranteed to grow at a compound 8.2% with a 10% bonus, she would have an income account valued at $358,758. That is what my clients did, and they will receive a 7-10% bonus and a compound growth rate of 6 - 8% of 110% of their original deposit until they plan to take their guaranteed lifetime income. As my clients look back over the prior year, do you think they remember the huge gains from 1996-2000 or 2003-2007? No. But they know they slept well during the disasters in 2000-2003 and the last few years, knowing that their money was locked-in and safe!

When we are looking to invest in financial products, we have to examine things for the long haul. We have to ask questions like *what is the average % yield over a certain period of time after fees and commissions?* In Cindy's case, the yield came out to zero or perhaps even negative over thirteen years. She might make back some of her money down the road and reclaim an average of 8 to 10% average annual return for her investment in stocks, but remember that an 8% annual gross yield is only 6% after the average annual mutual fund management and broker fees are deducted. A CD averaging 4-5% would have increased her money by 75% over thirteen years. A fixed indexed annuity would have given her a 7-8% annual gain (without management and broker fees) and more than doubled her money over thirteen years—without all the drama, worries, and headaches involved.

Therefore, Grace Advisory Group:Tax and Retirement Specialists promotes products that won't fall short of stock market performance over the long run and, unlike stocks, will provide you with positive and stable returns even in a down stock market. How can that be? Keep reading!

The Fourth Pillar: Lock In

The fourth and last financial pillar centers on the **lock-in mechanism that secures the growth of your account values to prevent losses during a future downturn**. What's the use of having growth on your investment if sometime in the future we hit a down cycle? What's the use of accumulating all those assets when you could lose it all when the music stops, and you don't get to a chair on time? That is why I like products with a lock-in mechanism that secures the gains and ensures that nothing is lost from year to year.

Remember Cindy's bumpy ride with her $100,000 from 1996 to 2009? With the **lock-in mechanism** of the fixed indexed annuity, she would have not given up her market gains when the sharp declines hit. Her accounts would flat line in a down year and go up in an up year. In fact, using real historic numbers of the S&P 500 index (the index in which Cindy would have participated), she would have doubled her money in thirteen years rather than breaking even with all the stress. Yes, she was only participating in 65 to 70% of the market gains—but none of its losses!

Strategies with Grace

After our discussion of the four pillars of a worry-free financial plan, I want to address some points to supplement your understanding of what we've been discussing.

I don't steer my clients into qualified retirement accounts like IRAs, 403(b)s, or 401(k)s—unless my client's company offers a match on my client's contributions into his/her retirement funds. In that case, I would say never exceed your company's contribution if the company has a policy that limits its own contribution. Why contribute more of your hard-earned money just for more risk? You should contribute just enough to get your company to put in its full share of its match—nothing more.

When I was young, I too was lured into putting money into tax-deferred plans. A small tax deduction today so that I could pay a much larger tax tomorrow (at retirement). I don't like having an IRS tax lien on my future pot of money—a lien that could substantially decrease my share of the pot for lifetime income as tax rates rise over the next five to ten years. Where do you think tax rates will be after the additional trillions of dollars that have been thrown at the Wall Street firms, banks, Fannie Mae, and Freddie Mac to keep them afloat? Up? Down? The same?

You know the answer! We have to pay for this deficit mess at some time in the future not to mention funding the huge deficits in Social Security, Medicare, and the looming healthcare crisis! Serving that current $14 trillion debt (and growing) means that tax revenues must increase.

I don't want to have my retirement future held hostage by the IRS when I know that down the road the tax I'll pay will far surpass the benefit I received from my contributions and accumulations.

Let's use an illustration. At forty-five years old, you put $10,000 into a supplemental retirement program—a 403(b), Deferred Comp 457, or 401(k) plan—after the employer match. You get an 8% return a year for twenty years from the supplemental savings program. Your employer and the government encourage you to do so because the core pension is likely going to be non-existent or at best inadequate to fund a retirement lifestyle equal in income to your working years.

The government gives you monetary incentives to put money into the supplemental program. The government says to you, "Put $10,000 in your retirement fund, and we're going to give you a $3,000 tax savings (assuming you are in a combined 30% federal and state tax bracket)." So it only costs you $7,000 a year to contribute $10,000. Your accumulated tax savings from the government would come to $60,000 over those twenty years ($3000 per year x 20 years). That sounds really attractive at first, doesn't it? Well, there are multiple ways we can look at this situation that might change your mind.

After twenty years, if you get 8% annual returns on your contributions, you would have accumulated $450,000. When you're sixty-five, you'll have some decisions to make. You always had your eye on that second home in the Carolinas or Tennessee. So you want to buy a house, and you cash in. To take your $450,000 out as income, you have to pay 42% in federal and state taxes. Before, you received a 30% tax benefit. Now taxes are higher because the lump sum distribution is ordinary income of $450,000 and thus taxed in a higher tax bracket.

So $450,000 minus 42% of $450,000 is $261,000, which is what you actually have in cash to buy your vacation dream home. You just sent the government an $189,000 "thank you" in one lump payment for their $60,000 tax benefit over the last twenty years. You should ask yourself one question: Whose retirement plan was this after all—mine or Uncle Sam's?

In another scenario, your tax advisor would tell you to take money out "the smart way" over the course of twenty years in retirement rather than a lump sum of $450,000 because you'll be killed in taxes as seen in the previous paragraph. Well, you follow their advice and take out $50,000 annually from your retirement fund from age sixty-six to eighty-five. Now when you withdraw $50,000 annually as income, you get charged 30% in taxes because $50,000 (plus all your other Social Security and other income) puts you in the 30% combined tax category. So each year you are charged $15,000 in taxes. Over twenty years of payouts, your tax bite grew to $300,000 ($15,000 x 20 years, doing it the "smart way!"). But your benefit from the government was still $60,000. Bad plan.

What is a better way to go? I tell people to pay the IRS its $3,000 a year while they're saving the $10,000 annually for twenty years and not take the government bait—I mean benefit. This way, your loss compared to the other scenarios is minimized. You only pay $60,000 in total taxes over the next twenty to forty years (age forty-five to eighty-five) instead of the much larger numbers in the above scenarios. Why does this make sense?

Well, originally our example showed that you have $10,000 to save per year. With my strategy, you gave $3,000 to the IRS, and now you have $7,000 to save for retirement. It's wiser to keep that $7,000 out of your supplemental retirement fund and choose between the following two strategies:

Strategy A:

Put $7,000 annually into a structured life insurance contract under current IRS parameters that will act like a supercharged Roth account without the IRS's age and income restrictions as to accessibility before age fifty-nine and a half. The benefit is that the buildup of your savings is tax free, meaning that if your savings bring in 5% returns this year, this 5% will not be taxed.

Another benefit is that withdrawing your money out of the life insurance cash account for pre-retirement emergencies or needs can also be tax free using loans under current tax law. If you die prior to your desired retirement age, there is a tax-free death benefit for your loved ones that will be substantially more than the after-tax amount of your qualified account.

The math also shows that your monthly income from the life insurance contract would provide an additional 40% more monthly income than the traditional qualified plan due to the tax-free loan provisions of the life policy—40% more income plus an enhanced death benefit that qualified plans don't give you!

You are able to achieve a comparable 8% annual return to the mutual funds in your qualified plan on the cash value of the life policy by using the same indexing strategy I use in the fixed indexed annuity, including the lock-in of future account values as you near retirement—without the mutual fund risk exposure!

Strategy B:

Put that $7,000 into investment real estate where you would receive the same tax benefits from depreciation and other expenses as contributing money to a qualified plan. However, you would get more control and flexibility over your money outside of the IRS's restrictions on qualified plans because you can refinance, sell, or hang on to the real estate property. If you have to choose between putting $1,000 in stocks or in real estate (with its leverage), it is better to put the money in real estate for the long haul. I would ask my clients to not give me $1,000 to put into a qualified plan or IRA and instead put it in real estate. Ten years down the road, when a downturn happens, you can still sell or refinance your real estate to survive, whereas you would have no control over your stocks shrinking in value.

Your accountant will confirm my numbers on the above illustrations because math is math, and the tax laws are what they are. He or she will not give advice about investments or real estate because they cannot be sure which investments or property purchases are the best for you or what your parameters are. So it is up to you to figure out personal parameters that would affect your real estate decisions on your own, using my advice of seeking balance and contentment for you and your family. We will continue our discussion of real estate and establishing contentment in later chapters.

Trillions of dollars have been thrown into the world economy for bailouts. Decades from now, Americans will likely be paying higher taxes to repay the cost of those bailouts. We need to be reminded that up until 1987, this country had marginal federal tax brackets as high as 70%—plus additional taxes in most states! That fact should get people scratching their heads and saying, "Tell us more about that," or "How did that happen, and will it happen again?" Remember earlier in the book? I explained the importance of your advisor understanding the taxes on your overall planning strategies. It's one of the reasons Grace Advisory Group: Tax and Retirement Specialists stands out from the pack—our team of specialists understands tax law in depth, drawing on many years of experience and training to minimize taxes wherever possible.

The strategies that I have shown work to save you money within all of today's tax laws and give you an idea of how to look at the numbers if tomorrow's tax laws change. The numbers that I shared with you are real. You can't refute them, and you can't argue with them. You must find better investment and savings strategies like SIPS to help you navigate the tax laws and in the end to be able to finance your retirement dreams.

chapter six

Money and the Pursuit of Happiness

Most of us think we can keep our work and personal lives separate. We think the way we invest and do business has nothing to do with the way we live or what we believe. As a result, people tend to depart from their comfort zone into the haze of uncertainty when they invest in an unfamiliar stock or business venture. In the end, the fruit of their investment or career choices often causes them and their family much heartache as they slide into a prison of debt or even bankruptcy.

When people are in financial trouble, they should say to themselves, "I'm going to change. I'm going to do a better job of handling my money." But many continue with the same investment and business habits that got them in trouble in the first place. How many people do you know who still have their money in stocks even though they lost almost half of their life savings in the recent financial meltdown? These same people are still in the game because with every new financial setback they are newly convinced by Wall Street that things are going to be better this time around. They buy into the fantasy economics that they can make back what they lost by doubling up at the casino's blackjack table.

But it's the same Wall Street system that failed them in 2008 and has failed them in the three years since, as hundreds of billions of dollars have been funneled into large and crumbling banks in an attempt to save Main Street. Yet Main Street is still suffering. If the cycle continues, then the next question on their minds will be, **"Why did I continue to listen to bad advice instead of changing my attitude about what is right for me?"**

Well, here's the simple answer to that question that I hope you never forget. We often fall for salesmanship when we are not focused on decision-making within our personal parameters. Someone who is articulate and persuasive convinces us that something is the "chance of a lifetime. You had better act now and not miss this opportunity." However, nothing is more plentiful than opportunities. The universe is crammed with thousands of opportunities.

You will never lack for an opportunity. It is your ability to focus and stay within your comfort zone that is paramount to your success. Remember when we Boomers thought thirty years ago that we would never be able to afford the home that our parents bought for $10,000 that had grown to $55,000? You know that house today is worth $500,000! Yeah, there will always be another opportunity.

In addition, many of us focus so much on our financial "stuff" or how our salary or job status stacks up against the next guy that we shift attention away from the more important things in life like our balance and relationships with our family and friends. When that happens, we become unhappy, stressed, and unsatisfied. We become motivated in life primarily by money and perceived success, often at the expense of violating our core values pertaining to people and spiritual growth. We don't have our hearts filled with inner peace as we claw for success and big bucks.

You've heard all of this before. And you know you want to find the right balance between work and your personal life. Take a look around you—are most of the people you know experiencing balance and contentment with their relationships, finances, and health? Remember my illustration in an earlier chapter depicting our relationships, finances, and health as the three legs of a stool called True Wealth. If one leg is weakened, the whole stool is going down with you on it!

So what can you do to get you there? What have successful people before you done to achieve balance and contentment? For the answers, let's examine the wisdom of King Solomon, someone who has been praised for 2,500 years by countless writers as one of the richest, wisest, and most successful kings in history. Yet with all his wealth, women, and success, he strived throughout his life to achieve that balance that we all are seeking. There's nothing really new about the financial strategies I talk about in this book: it's been around since the days of King Solomon. In this chapter, we will see how the system I've designed is founded upon Solomon's wisdom. I interpret Solomon's advice to be this:

1) *Understand who you are and what your personal boundaries are based on your interests, talents, and goals.*
2) *Clarify for yourself a philosophy of life and comfort zone about money, family, work, and retirement.*

What legacy will you leave your children when you leave this earth? Notice that I did not say *financial* legacy. I mean legacy as in the wisdom that you acquired in this life that you want to pass on to your heirs so they continue to bless others with their talents and gifts—a perpetual "Pay it Forward."

Your attitude concerning your desired legacy is very valuable to a financial strategist like me who is dedicated to helping you achieve financial success without violating the overall balance and contentment in your personal life. (Conversely, this information will *not* be important to a Wall Street bookie who's just trying to move you along to the next transaction). As a result, what you figure out about yourself based on Solomon's advice will help you be a better steward of your money and a better human being.

Wise and prudent investment decisions are the byproduct of setting the right goals and parameters. My clients and prospective clients need to know where they are right now—not just in terms of their financial lives but in terms of every aspect of their lives. Only then can we figure out where I'm going to take them. It starts with them, not me.

King Solomon wrote several volumes based on his pursuit of the best that he felt life had to offer. He described these pursuits in detail, and they are the same pursuits you and

I chase today. He labeled these vain interests **"futilities,"** as in "my vain pursuits to eat up this life just seem futile!" Let's examine their relevance.

The futility of pursuing happiness by the endless gathering of knowledge

Sometimes, gathering knowledge is a cumbersome and frustrating task. It's a time- and energy-consuming research process to try to know everything about finances, politics, religion, health, and on and on! It's much better to *narrow the boundaries of knowledge* for your specific needs and interests rather than to live with a restless guilt trip for not knowing enough facts to be a big winner on TV's *Jeopardy* or worse yet—to not have all the answers to everyone's problems or questions.

Knowledge is a seed to an understanding for a solution in some area of your life. You must focus your valuable time and energy on obtaining knowledge that is specific to your needs, interests, and experience, so that you can plant that seed of knowledge in your future. You know—we only have so much mental bandwidth before information overload starts to affect our decision-making process—paralysis by analysis, if you will.

Here's a case study of why trying to know too much about too many topics can leave you dazed and confused instead of healthy, wealthy, and wise. You had $600,000 in your investment account, but after the recent financial crisis, you're down to $400,000. You're joking with your friends (although there's nothing really funny about it) that your 401(k) has shrunk to the size of a 201(k).

You're not sure if you'll have a job during the next five years, let alone the next five months! In this situation, you shouldn't be reading books about flipping real estate for a quick profit or venturing into multi-level marketing or any other kind of risky investment strategies of which you know nothing. It doesn't make sense for you now to watch some salesman on TV talking about the next quickest but riskiest way to make a buck. It will be a waste of your time. What would Solomon say? He'd say the endless gathering of information in areas outside your understanding and expertise is ultimately futile. Think about commodities like gold and silver. You can't buy a gallon of milk or a loaf of bread at the 7-Eleven with gold bullion bars or bars of silver!

Furthermore, you don't need Wall Street firms to tell you to double down on the mutual fund blackjack table to make up all of what you have lost. You have received some bad advice in the past, and you don't need any more guesswork in an attempt for a quick, risky turnaround at the risk of even more devastating losses.

Solomon would tell you that it's normal to make emotional decisions when it comes to money, especially when you are in panic mode for losing a large chunk of your retirement nest egg and feel the need to recover quickly. But you always need to go back to your personal boundaries and examine where you are and where you need to go. You may have a family and other responsibilities that require you to be more conservative in your decision-making. Yes, you've lost $200,000, but the pipedream of making that money back with high-risk bets should not be on your mind right now. You might lose another $200,000! Then where will you be?

What is important now is hanging on to what you have left and ensuring that it grows back safely and securely. You need to consult experienced financial advisors like myself or read books like the one you're holding to obtain information about how to keep what you have for your family's future since you can't afford to lose.

Another fatal mistake is to take the advice of a well meaning friend or family member. Unless they are trained and certified (proper designations) to offer financial advice, safe money advice, their free advice will be the most expensive advice you will ever receive.

The only people who really "get rich quick" are the people who are still pulling down the insanely high salaries and bonuses at your expense on that street of dreams in Lower Manhattan—Wall Street.

The futility of pursuing happiness by accumulating vast possessions

We think we need to have more houses, cars, vacations, and investment properties because society says so. We are told that we need to make more money in order to buy more stuff to make us happy or to fulfill our sense of **what we are** and **what we possess.** We do this at the expense of our spiritual contentment founded on **who we are** and **who motivates us** to do our best in service to others. This bombardment of material vanity has resulted from the explosion of today's media from its continual stream of promotions and advertisements via the Internet, television, radio, and magazines.

The media feeds the common misconception that money and things will make you happy. But the truth is, as long as you are pursuing money, you are inflicted with a disease I call "Wanting More." What are the symptoms? The need to acquire possessions that do not enhance our life one bit; and the restlessness and emptiness experienced when those newly acquired possessions fail to provide satisfaction and fulfillment. We think the "cure" is taking on more risk in our investments in order to get more return to pay for more material goods. We also experience pressure and stress, always pushing ourselves to work harder to make more money. Nothing is more unsettling than the exchange of the short-term thrill for the long-term anxiety of owning that luxury car you really didn't need and can't afford.

I have a different standard for wealth. The cure for the restlessness most of us feel when the "stuff" just doesn't fulfill us like we thought it would is a pill called "Enough!" We'll be very satisfied with our life if we keep a decent job that allows us to pay our basic budget needs for the month, while providing some extra savings for our retirement future and needed vacations to recharge. I don't care how much money you make over time—no matter if you are a baseball player, a corporate executive, or a utility lineman—if you put 5% to 10% of your income away each year and don't lose the gains you have accumulated, you will be able to live comfortably when you retire. You won't have a second home in Maui or the wallet-emptying sports car that just wasn't necessary for a comfortable lifestyle. But you can rest assured that your working years will be spent in contentment, and more contentment will await you when you arrive at retirement!

The futility of pursuing happiness from work devoid of passion

A teacher may feel completely satisfied with their job because they enjoy serving the educational and emotional needs of their students. Some people might, however, try to sway our teachers into doing something else in order to make more money. People who don't understand the inherent satisfaction that this educator enjoys might ask, "Why don't you get into multi-level marketing or real estate? Why experience all the stress of dealing with kids when you can get into this industry for two years and be set for the rest of your life?"

I think it would be futile for a passionate teacher to switch to another profession just for more money. Anything other than teaching is not the calling or assignment for his or her life and won't keep them energized to be of service. If they don't enjoy doing something, they are most likely going to be mediocre at it, which means that they will exchange their mental health and contentment for a few extra bucks pursuing a career that was outside their assignment.

People who focus on exercising their passion in their career choices over how much money they'll make seem to be the happiest people I know. On the other hand, in my experience, people who pursue money as the primary motive for pursuing a career at the neglect of their passions are restless and miserable. How about those who must take a job outside their passions and fields of interest in order to make a living? Well, I would tell them to continue with their day jobs but find an outlet for their passions outside that job to stay happy and content.

We all have a chance at any time to look at the year that we have ahead of us and say to ourselves, "What is it that I really want? What can I do to gain more knowledge about what I am interested in? How can I be a better steward of my money from now on?" You can be seventy years old or older and still follow your passion and desire to bless others as you write the script for your remaining years here on Earth.

Now imagine that you have passed away and are in a casket at your own funeral. You are able to hear everything people say about you. Do you like what you hear? You realize that people talk **less** about your business and your wealth and **more** about what you meant to them, what you did for them, and how you enhanced the lives of all who came in contact with you.

People honor integrity, not wealth, unless they are too self-absorbed and empty to recognize integrity. Lee Iacocca, the former head of Chrysler, wrote something in his first book that struck me as extremely profound. He said that he has never run across a friend who had accumulated great wealth and who on his deathbed would say something like, "Lee, I wish I spent more time at the office." It's the people we pour our lives into that matter in the end, not the extra million bucks earned at the expense of our most important assets—our family and friends. Focus on the things that remain in eternity!

If your life is properly balanced among finances, relationships, and health, you will be more motivated and inspired to pick up the pieces and rebuild when challenges or catastrophes arise. How can balanced people successfully do this again and again, while others put a gun to their heads when they lose it all on stupid investments or at the Wall Street casino window called "wanting more"? The person who has true wealth focuses on ***who he is***, not what he is or has. He knows that he is a person with a family, friends, and a passion for doing something he loves. A person's self-worth is not determined by what they have earned or attained but by the value they have brought to the lives of people they have served.

True contentment follows our self-evaluation of what activities bring us the most excitement and fulfillment. The answer to that question will put us on the road to contentment in our lives' labor. The level of wealth you attain in this life is determined by your ability to enhance the lives of others through your service or products created that solve their problems. Great servants make great leaders, and great servants attain great wealth. Great wealth is only partially measured by the number of zeroes at the end of your net worth statement. Remember, who do you want to eulogize you—-your friends and family, or your banker and accountant?

The futility of pursuing happiness from money

Anybody who loves money more than anything else will never be satisfied with the balance in his or her bank account. Everybody who craves abundance will never have enough. That's why King Solomon said, "When a person's income or wealth increases, then people's consumption of things increase." They buy more things when they make $100,000 compared to when they made $50,000. Many people tend to spend more than they make. They don't grasp the concept of "Enough!"

Let's take an example. Gene ran a successful business for thirty years and sold it for several million dollars; now he is very popular in the cocktail party circuit. He's constantly being hit up to join new business opportunities from his new "friends" at the top. Everybody's got a deal, and everybody's trying to get everybody else in their deals.

Gene forgets the four pillars and jumps into an investment without sufficient **knowledge or**

understanding of the principles behind the venture or the details of the business in which he just invested his hard-earned money. He lost **control** of his money when he gave it to someone else before setting his personal and financial boundaries on the limit of acceptable loss that would not affect his family's financial and relational well-being. Does that sound safe to you? I hope not!

We also have examples of athletes or entertainers who in their careers have made millions of dollars and ended up with nothing in just a few years after their careers end. One day we read that they made $20 million in a year and the next day they declare bankruptcy. How did that happen? Well, they've spent beyond their means. They were influenced by people around them who didn't care whether they could afford to lose money or not. Gene and these athletes are examples of the **folly of riches**—the folly that happens when the pursuit of riches overtakes common sense and balance.

Remember, feeling rich is a subjective emotion. A $100,000 salary is considered a fortune for the man who makes $25,000 a year living in a small town in the Midwest, while that salary would be many steps down the ladder for a New York executive who makes $500,000 annually.

Don't get me wrong: I'm not saying that money is a bad thing. The *obsession* over money is the bad thing—better known as greed!

James Stovall's *The King's Legacy* is a book about a king's desire to pass on a personal legacy called the Wisdom of the Ages that would have a long-term impact on the lives of his subjects and their descendants beyond temporal things, such as coins and monuments. In the book, the king invites several professionals—a banker, a professor, and a farmer—to counsel him about the wisdom they have gleaned from their lives. I could relate to the banker in the story, who stated that money is neither good nor bad; it's a tool that can be used to build or destroy. He told the king he had learned that if you are not content in your present financial state, no amount of money would change or enhance your outlook on life.

How do you know that **you** are content? Check your credit card statements! This advice is a lesson learned from our discussion of the futility of accumulating vast possessions: As long as you are obsessed with accumulating more and more possessions (and usually you could do without them just fine), you are afflicted by a disease called "More." The banker reminded the king that money is not the key to wealth; **knowledge** of your assignment on earth to bless others with your talents is the key to wealth.

With everything we do, we must do it with contentment. Why is this concept of contentment important when it comes to making the right investment decisions? Too often we fool ourselves that we are going to make a lot of money with our investment decisions, yet we fail to see that those decisions are driven by worry, greed, or fear. We must be honest with ourselves about our boundaries for risk tolerance as well as determining whether our goals are formed out of a mindset of "Enough!" or "More." We must find the right people to help us work within the boundaries and mindsets that we have set for ourselves; only then will fear and greed no longer control us. We'll be taking direction from King Solomon and not from the King worshiped on Wall Street—His Royal Highness, Greed!

chapter seven

The Truth about Home Equity Management

Most Americans have their financial net worth tied up in two large assets: their homes and their retirement accounts. We rely on this combination to provide us with a pot of money to survive on in our later years. You have probably received advice to pay off your home mortgages as quickly as possible. The idea is that rather than being burdened with house payments at retirement, you'll just sit comfortably on the front porch of your home worry free. However, is having a house free and clear of debt the best way to go?

No. And here's why.

In his best-selling book *Missed Fortune 101*, retirement strategist Douglas Andrew states: "The most important elements of home equity management are maintaining liquidity; safety of principal and creating the opportunity for home equity to grow in a separate side fund, where it is accessible in the event of an emergency:"

For example, a couple came into my office and asked me to give them counsel on the largest investment of their lifetime. They said to me, "Help us retire securely. What kind of an investment should we make?" Then I gave them some features of an investment that they might consider as follows: 1) you can determine the amount of money you put into it; 2) you can set up a schedule of future investment contributions; 3) you can contribute more each month than what's originally scheduled; 4) all the money you put into the investment, however, is not liquid and not safe from loss; 5) this investment earns no returns; 6) your income tax liability will increase with each contribution; and 7) finally, when this investment plan is complete, it would not pay you a dime of income for your retirement. Now I ask them, "Sound good to you?"

"Of course not," says the husband. "Who in the heck would make such an investment? There is no liquidity, flexibility, rate of return, or tax advantages. It's against the four pillars of financial planning you talked about, Bob."

Then the wife tugs the husband's sleeve and says to him, "Honey, doesn't that kind of sound like our mortgage?"

Is a Mortgage Good or Bad?

A mortgage is a loan from the bank to finance the purchase of your home. It's bad because of all the reasons my previous example pointed out. Plus, with any kind of loan, there is interest. No one likes to pay interest. Therefore, everyone thinks that the mortgage is your foe because it is debt, and "debt" is an ugly word. Because we think mortgage is bad, many financial advisors advise their clients to invest in homes using the "get-rid-of-mortgage-ASAP" strategy. The myth is that this strategy is the best investment for your retirement.

The truth is that the mortgage does more good than you know. Not only does it help you finance your home, but it helps finance your retirement. I'm going to show you how the mortgage is actually your friend.

The big thing to realize here is that there are two kinds of debt: preferred debt and non-preferred debt. Preferred debt is debt you should have because it gives you safety, liquidity, and a rate of return. The tax advantage you would get on the preferred debt is just the icing on the cake since preferred debt is tax deductible.

Non-preferred debt is the avoid-at-all-costs debt. It is debt owed to credit card companies and other institutions that charge an extremely high amount of interest like 10-20%. You can't deduct non-preferred debt. It costs more to stay in non-preferred debt than in preferred debt. You are better off going into preferred debt to pay off your credit card balance.

I put mortgages in the preferred debt category. For example, you want to buy a $500,000 house. You put $100,000 or 20% of the purchase price down and take out a $400,000 mortgage from the bank for your house. The bank will charge you about 5% as an interest rate. The first advantage of mortgages is tax deduction. You are in the 30% tax bracket, so after the tax deduction, you really pay a 3.5% interest rate to the bank. In other words, if you have a $2,200 monthly mortgage payment, you really pay $1,540 to the bank because of your 30% tax deduction. That's a really good deal.

Uncle Sam has become my partner because he helps to defray the cost of borrowing for me by giving me a tax advantage. He's giving me a tax incentive to buy a house in order to boost the economy and give jobs to realtors, builders, contractors, etc. Our economy has gone down the drain recently partly in response to a real estate depression that terminated many housing-related jobs.

I never want people to pay interest on their investments just to get a tax deduction. People shouldn't go into debt unless there is a good reason to do so. I'm going to show you that the reason to have a mortgage goes beyond the advantage of tax deductions.

The Arbitrage System

The prevalent myth nowadays says there are two kinds of people in the world: those who earn interest and those who pay interest. People who earn interest go to the bank, put $100,000 in a CD, and get 2% returns on their money. Others pay interest on the loans they take out to start a business or to buy a house.

I say there is a third person out there who both pays interest and earns interest. The interesting thing is: they earn interest at a higher rate than the interest rate they are paying. They are their own banker. They do what banks, credit unions, and merchant banks have done for centuries; that is, borrow money at a lower rate of interest and invest it to earn a higher interest rate.

Like the big banks, this third person understands the power of using other people's money. In the banks' case, they make money with your money. For instance, you go to a local bank, put $100,000 on a CD, and get a 2% return for the next year. You think the bank's just going to put your $100,000 in a vault? And it's just paying you 2% because they feel good about having extra money in the vault? No! They will loan the money at a 5 to 8% interest rate to someone who is buying a house or a car or a 10-30% interest rate to someone who is paying for things by credit card and so on. The bank desires to make at least 2-3% annually on your money. That doesn't sound like much but think about all the people who would give $100,000 to the bank. Their contributions add up to billions of dollars of deposits for the bank. The bank makes a profit by loaning out the billions. This system is called "arbitrage."

Arbitrage is a system that gives you profit based on the difference between what you pay in interest and what you earn in interest. With arbitrage, you borrow at one rate and invest at another rate. In addition to banks, insurance companies also follow this system when they sell you annuities. That is why banks and insurance companies are among the wealthiest institutions in the world. (I'm talking about reputable banks and not the small banks that have failed in the recent economy for making bad loans.)

Having a mortgage also allows you to take advantage of the arbitrage system. You can take out a mortgage with an interest rate of 4% and invest the money that you otherwise would have put into the house in a fixed indexed annuity to collect returns of 6%. In the end, you will collect positive returns from your investments from borrowing at a net 2.4% and receiving 4.2% after tax considerations. If you pay cash for the house in the beginning, you will not be able to collect this kind of arbitrage.

Moreover, if you try to pay off your mortgage as quickly as possible, you put yourself at the mercy of the banker. Let me explain: Let's say you are thinking about paying extra each month on your mortgage. What if you pay $3,000 instead of the set $2,200 this month? You are basically saying to the bank, "Here, Mr. Banker, here's an extra $800 that I don't need. You can take it, and don't bother to pay me interest for it. If I need this money back, I'll come to you, and borrow it on your terms by proving to you that I can afford to borrow my own money." Sound ridiculous? Well, that's exactly what that transaction entails.

With the above example, you lose control of the $800—money that you could use as emergency money in the future to pay the bank mortgage. When you pay the bank that extra money, you don't get any extra tax advantages. If you lose your job or a member of your family gets sick in the future, you won't have this $800 anymore to use. You will be forced to go to the bank to borrow back this money. You will have to deal with all of the bank's tedious procedures in order to get this money back. Plus, you will have to pay interest on the new loan that you take out. You were better off not paying that extra $800 to the bank in the first place and instead putting that money in a rainy-day fund.

The Importance of Liquidity

Nothing beats having cash on hand during gloomy economic times. If you lose your job, get divorced, or get sick, it will really be a tragedy that you don't have liquid assets. You would be forced to liquidate assets like your house or car—you would have to sell them for cash at fire-sale prices. On the other hand, people who have cash liquidity can slide by emergencies, meet their expenses, and do grocery shopping, unlike the people without liquid assets. Taking out a mortgage and not trying to repay it as fast as you can, will give you emergency cash by separating it from your house or removing it from your backyard as I like to say.

Let's look at this example: Tom and John are both age fifty, have good jobs, and can afford a mortgage. They both inherited $500,000 in cash and are both looking to buy $500,000 houses. John chose to put up $500,000 for his house while Tom only put down $100,000 for his house and borrowed the remaining $400,000. From 2007-2009, the real estate market went down, and home property values experienced losses of up to 50-60% in manufacturing states like Indiana, Ohio, Michigan, and New Jersey. In Naples, Florida, where they live, the $500,000 homes that Tom and John have went down "only" 30% in value to $350,000. Whose financial condition is now better (or less bad): no-loan John who put every dime he had in his home, or Tom, who put $100,000 down and took out a $400,000 loan?

Obviously, after the market downturn, Tom is in a better financial situation because he has that $400,000 in safe savings to support him in case of emergencies, while John doesn't. If John lost his job and is in major financial need, he might be forced to go to his banker to borrow money. John will say to him, "Look, I'm free and clear of any mortgage. Can I get a loan for these tough times?" The banker doesn't care that John doesn't owe anything. All the banker cares about is whether John can repay the loan.

Without any liquid assets or a job, it doesn't look like John can, even though he's got a house free and clear. If the bank rejects his loan application, John's credit score would go down because he could no longer afford his car payment, etc. He would be forced to sell his house in a down market for $350,000 when he had bought it for $500,000. The house might not even sell right away and who knows how long he has to wait to get the cash from the sale.

In contrast to no-loan John, loaner Tom took the extra $400,000 that he didn't put into his house and invested some of it using a Sequential Income Portfolio System I designed. His investment generates 6% annual cash flow, and his mortgage only carries a 3.5% interest rate after tax savings. Therefore, taking into consideration his mortgage, Tom actually has a 2.5% excess cash flow on the money he didn't put into his house. Tom is taking full advantage of the arbitrage system. Plus, if he's ever in need of cash, he can just tap some of the extra cash that he's got in his safe income account, all the while having had the extra cash flow to enhance his retirement lifestyle.

Now someone might say, "Great, I get it; the better man here is loaner Tom. But aren't we missing the fact that Tom's got a mortgage payment of $2,200 each month while John doesn't?" Well, I would answer that let's not forget that Tom is really only paying $1,540 for his mortgage each month because of his tax deductions. But more to the point, would you rather make the $1,540 payment each month with hundreds of thousands of liquid and safe assets or make no payment a month but be lacking in cash in case of emergency? Remember that both had jobs and could afford a mortgage.

The above is our basic discussion of mortgages. We will move on to talking about home equity in general. Let's discuss the features of a prudent investment and if home equity measures up to these features. The features of a prudent investment are safety, liquidity, flexibility, decent rate of return, and tax advantages. I say home equity doesn't have any of the above features. Let's talk about these features one by one.

How Safe Is Your Home Equity?

Home equity is defined as the difference between the market value of the house and the value of the loan (market value minus loan value). If the value of your house is $500,000 and you have $400,000 in mortgages, your home equity is $100,000.

If you have a house paid free and clear, and you experience a flat real estate market for ten years, your home equity would stay the same without gains or losses. However, if you experience a market loss of 30-50% (and these numbers are based on reality), then your home equity would be significantly reduced. You just saw the largest asset you own depreciate. Therefore, it's not safe to put all your money in the house. Home equity is not safe from market attacks.

How Liquid Is Your Home Equity?

Irene is seventy-six years old and has two houses. Her house on Sanibel Island has decreased 15% in value but is still worth about $2 million today. Her other house in Deep Lagoon Marina is worth $300,000. She has less than $20,000 in the bank—period! Her total income is less than $30,000.

Irene is old school since she lived through the Depression. She thinks that if she puts a loan on the house, then she is more likely to lose it. As of now, she only makes $2,000 of rental income from the Sanibel property—which is below market standards—but that's good enough for her. She only earns about 1% annual returns from her real estate each year, taxable as regular income rates. In addition, she is responsible for the repairs and maintenance of her houses. Irene sees her house-rich and cash-poor situation with her houses as good post-depression economic planning.

What if Irene has $2.3 million worth of real estate assets and she went to her friendly banker and said to him, "I got all this money buried in my backyard and I have an emergency requiring $200,000 in cash. Will you lend me $200,000?"? The bank would reject her because she had insufficient liquidity and income to pay back the loan. She even says, "Heck, I can use some of the $200,000 to pay you back if needed." The answer is still NO. If she needed cash, she would have to sell her properties with huge tax consequences. The lesson from Irene is that home equity isn't liquid and is usually unable to meet your emergency needs when and if you need money.

What's the Rate of Return on Your Home Equity?

If you bought a house in 2005 for $500,000, and it is worth $350,000 today, you not only received a 0% rate of return, but you experienced a 30% loss. The traditional real estate market experiences a 20 to 30% loss every decade or so. It's all a game of supply and demand; when the demand decreases, the prices fall. It takes about ten years to make up a 30% loss. The value of your house will have to grow 43% in order to get back to its purchase price. And it's not easy to climb back through a depressed real estate market. We're not even sure how long it will take to flush out the bad loans and the extra supply of homes (due to the lack of ability to buy) in the recent market.

From my analysis of over sixty years of historical data on real estate cycles, it usually takes about six to eight years to get from the bottom of the real estate market to its peak. When can you expect a point of return in these years? The math is simple: Your house was valued at $500,000 in 2005. In 2009, it is valued at $350,000. In 2015, or possibly later in this environment, more than likely - the value will come back to $500,000. And how much did you make during those ten plus years? The answer is zero.

Home Equity Loans

Want to create more liquidity for your assets or put more cash in your pocket? Besides taking out a mortgage when you first purchased the house, you can borrow against your home equity by taking out a home equity loan from the bank.

I see scenarios like this all the time: A retired couple in their seventies has a lovely $500,000 home off McGregor Boulevard paid free and clear, and their only sources of income are around $35,000 from Social Security and approximately $25,000 from one spouse's qualified plan, or $60,000 annually—pretty good income, as long as one of them doesn't die or their nest egg doesn't lose money! They also have $50,000 in a bank CD. They have no other liquidity than their retirement plan.

One evening, the couple is taking a moonlit stroll under the stately palm trees when the husband collapses. He dies from a heart attack a few hours later. The Social Security income to his widow is reduced to $25,000 annually from $35,000. As fate would have it, the retirement plan value that was around $200,000 a few years ago has been deflated by 30% to $140,000 by the last three years of stock market performance and over withdrawing from the retirement account ($25,000 ÷ 140,000 = 17.8%). She was counting on the $25,000 income payout for another ten years, but it will only last five to six years, if it doesn't lose any more value. And her $500,000 home has now gone down 30% to $350,000. "What happened," she cries. "And what is going to happen to me?"

Well, now we have a widow in her seventies running out of money before she runs out of life! Can Wall Street help her? Will her kids help her? She is stressed worrying about decreasing income and increasing expenses over the next ten to twenty years. What would Grace Advisory Group: Tax and Retirement Specialists do for her?

We would bring her hope and encouragement!

Step I: We would have her get her retirement plan money ($140,000) out of risk and into a structured income portfolio system (SIPS) and combine it with Step II.

Step II: We would have her take out a $140,000 (40% of appraised value) reverse mortgage on her home (no widow in her seventies wants to sell her home and move away from her comfort zone).

Step III: Combine the $140,000 retirement plan money and the $140,000 from the reverse mortgage (total $280,000) into a 6% SIPS paying her $16,800 per year for life. A total of $41,800 for life. Not as good as $60,000, but she won't run out of money in five years.

Step IV: We would have her keep the $50,000 FDIC-guaranteed CD at her bank for emergency liquidity. Her home value more than likely will be higher in fifteen years for added income and liquidity if she lives longer than age ninety.

What was the result of this plan? She now has the $25,000 Social Security income, plus the $16,800 from the SIPS plan. She won't run out of money in five years or worry about having to live on only $25,000 in her eighties. And she doesn't have to depend on her kids helping her with expenses. She is thrilled with Grace Advisory Group: Tax and Retirement Specialists.

And this is a true story!

In Addition to Real Estate, the 401(k)

Let's say, optimistically, that you have $1 million in your 401(k). If you take money out of it, it's fully taxable. You might be sixty-five years old and plan to take $75,000 out annually for the rest of your life. But if it's not in a SIPS or another guaranteed investment strategy, who's to say that million dollars won't turn into $500,000 overnight?

It's the old primary need of the return **of** your money not just return **on** your money.

Let me ask you a question: In light of all the trillions of dollars thrown overboard to rescue the passengers of the sinking ship "USS Wall Street," do you think income and estate taxes will go up, down, or stay the same over the next five to ten years? If you are a company that needs to increase cash flow to survive, and all things being equal, do you need to lower revenues or increase revenues? There's your answer as to where taxes are heading.

For the large number of Americans who are reading this book, you will be retiring on Social Security and pension income—either from a defined benefit plan (core retirement plan of company, state, or government) or a defined contribution plan (in which you contributed to a 401(k), 403(b), 457, IRA, or deferred comp. to supplement your other income sources). If your income from all sources exceeds $35,000, most of it will be taxed. If the taxable income exceeds $69,000 as a couple (or $34,500 if single), you are in the federal 25% tax bracket in 2011.

So let's say you've done a pretty good job at saving, and you have a good pension from the state, government, or company; plus you have Social Security and income off other investments. Let's also assume you are in the 30% combined federal and state bracket and have $600,000 in your supplemental plan (401(k), IRA, 403B, etc.). Taking that $75,000 out would give you a net $52,500 to spend because of a 30% tax bill.

What happens if you are taxed 50% when taxes increase? Then you would only have $35,000 to spend—your lifestyle will be greatly affected. The point is that the 401(k) is not reliable, as it is an IRS lien on your retirement future, and you don't know the particulars of the lien as the rules can and will change over the next twenty years. How it's taxed, when it's available without penalty, and other yet-to-be-disclosed tax law changes are potentially on the horizon. This is the danger of having only a 401(k) or other fully taxable pension plan as your primary source of income and a paid-up home where the equity provides no additional income to you as taxes and inflation tears into your retirement lifestyle.

I'm a big advocate of reverse mortgages for those people who have all their retirement strategy tied up in their qualified plans and home equity and who face a possible reduction of their lifestyles when (not if) taxes increase. Many people have lost a significant portion of their nest egg over the past three years. I suggest to people who are over sixty-two years old and who have at least 70% equity in their properties to look at reverse mortgages to provide a significant increase in their retirement incomes to make up for reductions from taxes, market losses, and potential medical expenses. Have your cake and eat it, too.

Using a SIPS strategy, you can receive a cash flow from the proceeds of the reverse mortgage while preserving all or most of your principal for the kids. Let Grace Tax show you how to retire with Grace.

The only limitation to this move is that for a couple, the youngest spouse has to be at least sixty-two years old. All you have to do is to call your bank and ask for a reverse mortgage on your house. Such a move requires no payment to the bank, no qualifying or out-of-pocket expenses; all you need is to keep your property taxes and insurance current. Note that your family or the state has one year after your death to either sell the house to repay the loan you took out or refinance the house and keep it.

Let's look at a couple of examples on how this strategy greatly helped a couple of my clients. Janet is seventy-six and has her primary home on Marco Island; it was worth $500,000 in 2007, but by the summer of 2008, it dropped to $300,000 as the real estate bubble started to deflate. She had less than $20,000 to her name and lived on Social Security and some of her husband's pension, totaling less than $17,000 annually.

I had her take out a $120,000 (40%) reverse mortgage to provide additional liquidity to protect her from further declines in her home equity. In her case and in the majority of cases I review for retired folks, having a home paid off is wonderful, as long as you have sufficient income to maintain a decent lifestyle comparable to how you lived before retirement.

The interesting sideline to the story: Janet's home value decreased over the past fifteen months to $225,000, but she has all her equity out and no payments. If she had not acted to get the $120,000 out last year to ensure adequate liquidity, she would only be able to get out $90,000 today. She doesn't care what her home is worth—she just knows that she has money for her needs and peace of mind.

Here's another example where a reverse mortgage would make sense. A retired couple (age seventy-five) has a home in the Bonita Bay gated community valued at $750,000 in 2007 with a $200,000 mortgage. Their mortgage payment is $2,200 per month. They do not have much liquidity other than a diminished 401(k) account after Wall Street finished with them. By October 2009, the home dropped in value to $500,000, and the retired owner still has mortgage payments on $200,000.

This retired couple should look at a reverse mortgage for about $200,000 to pay off that $200,000 mortgage (and save the $2,200 monthly payment).

But what about the children and the estate, you might ask? It's always the kids who complain to their parents who take out mortgages and reverse mortgages as this move affects their future inheritance. Well, I say to those kids that unless they are willing to write a $2,200 monthly check to Mom and Dad's retirement for the rest of their lives, **stop complaining**. Of course, asking that these kids shell out their own money to pay for their parents' expenses might be asking for too much! Or see us about a SIPS strategy and have your cake and eat it, too.

The Difference between Wall Street and Grace Advisory Group: Tax and Retirement Specialists

There is a lot of misinformation and abuse when it comes to the way people are advised to manage their home equity. Insurance agents who sell risky variable annuities and the Wall Street bookies cannot talk to seniors about the proper management of home equity to create safety, liquidity, and a rate of return to enhance their lifestyles. Most financial advisors don't have the patience and integrity to advise people to put away 10-15% of their money into CDs as there is no commission on CDs. I believe you have to create a proper blend between annuities and CDs so that any short-term liquidity needs are met during the first three to five years of your plan.

The problem in this country is that very few super wealthy people (less than 5% of the general populace) can afford the risk associated with stock investments. There are too many Wall Street brokers and insurance company agents chasing them down with the "hard sell" process. As a result, the sales guys have to go after people who can't afford the risk.

When there is no longer enough wealth to serve the top, the financial industry pushes risk downward onto the masses. After eating the big fish, they go after the smaller fish and leave no meat on the bones. This Wall Street strategy is born out of necessity and greed. As a result, many people who should not have been targeted by Wall Street were. Wall Street has their eyes set on the 401(k) market because the average Joes don't have that much money outside their 401(k)s. Because the 401(k) is so ubiquitous, Joe is left with little choice but to go along with the risk that Wall Street feeds him.

On the other hand, the Wall Street broker could care less about the senior citizen with $2 million in equity on his house and little liquid assets to invest. The senior might as well be homeless and pushing a shopping cart! They don't care about you unless you have liquid assets to risk. Without liquid assets, you are just not their target market. But you still have significant assets to manage and secure in your real estate equity—usually your largest single asset.

Grace Advisory Group: Tax and Retirement Specialists was created to be a counterforce to these Wall Street salesmen and help people who can't afford to lose money. I have stories upon stories from the people I have helped.

The economy had collapsed around them, and their portfolios had gone down with it. They are thrilled that they have extra income from the mortgage strategies that I have shown them.

Remember the two fifty-year-old gents earlier in the chapter (Tom and John)? When Tom followed my advice, he only put $100,000 down for a $500,000 home, got a $400,000 mortgage that he could afford, had a partner in Uncle Sam (tax savings on mortgage interest), and invested $400,000 into our safe fixed indexed annuity that offered an 8% bonus and is guaranteed to grow at an 8% compound growth rate until age 85. In fifteen years at age sixty-five, he accumulated $1,370,377. That $1,370,377 would pay him out a $75,371 annual income for the rest of his life - on top of his 401(k), Social Security, and other income.

I would take that $75,371 and pay the $26,400 annual mortgage for the year ($2,200 x 12). After he makes the mortgage payments, he would have **$48,971 left over** to enjoy that he wouldn't have had if his house was paid off. With the properly designed retirement plan, he will have liquidity, flexibility, and peace of mind during his working years, and $48,971 additional income for the rest of his life. By leaving the money out of his backyard, he grew his "repositioned" equity for fifteen years and has enough money to cover his mortgage for the rest of his life—sounds like a paid-off house to me, *without* the risk of losing equity buried in the backyard!

For every person who doesn't understand the importance of safety, liquidity, and rate of return on your real estate equity, I have found three who get it. If you don't feel comfortable following my advice, yet you believe in the math, please tell your friends and family to visit the gracetax.com website or have them give us a call. Helping others with their retirement planning is part of the good-old sowing and reaping life philosophy.

A Final Word

Real estate entails risk. So when you do buy additional real estate, do so according to your budget. Put as little down as possible and keep your money liquid in a side pot to cover unforeseen emergencies, repairs, and cash flow needs. Never put every dime you have in a house, the stock market, or a limited partnership. That way, you will be able to handle potential financial emergencies caused by a lack of control of your money.

chapter eight

How Grace Advisory Group: Tax and Retirement Specialists Can Help You

Now that you've seen all the problems that traditional, high-risk Wall Street-style investing entails, you may be asking, "How do I get started on moving my money to safer ground? And who can help me do that?" As someone who has shown you what a brighter day can look like for your retirement, I'm not going to leave you standing in the rain.

The retirement planning industry uses two ways to find clients: the "hard sell" process and the "buy when ready" process. Wall Street only uses the "hard sell" process. Here's how it works:

Step 1)

Without a clue about your retirement options, you walk into an asset management firm—we could call it Schwab or Fidelity, but we could just as easily call it Gambling With Your Money, Inc. Or they may call themselves fee-only money managers. Always ask what credentials they have. You are entitled to ask, "Do you have the training and education necessary to accomplish *my* financial goals, not yours?"

You are relying on someone to guide you in the right direction. You figure that since these people are wearing nice suits and working out of nice offices, they must know what they're talking about. Of course, they don't, but that doesn't stop them from talking or their prospects from believing what they're told.

Step 2)

Upon the advice of an advisor at Gambling With Your Money, Inc., you invest in stocks, or stock/bond mutual funds. It doesn't matter what kind of person you are, whether you're rich or middle class or old, young, or somewhere in the middle. As long as you have the money to invest, Wall Street advisors will sell you the same products. Those products are usually stock mutual funds and bond funds. Why? If you've read this far into the book, you know the answer: Those "investments" make the investment bookies and their casinos the most money.

The "hard sell" process takes place anytime Wall Street can take advantage of your lack of knowledge, understanding, or control. It's like walking into a Best Buy without knowing what kind of TV you want to buy, and suddenly the salesman is in your face with a deal for anything from a small HD TV to a complete $10,000 home entertainment system! The salesperson might end up trying to sell the high-end stuff when your needs and budget don't call for that product. But it's not the salesman's fault that you walked into the store completely unprepared and uneducated concerning your needs. Can you see the similarity in how most people buy their investments that will supposedly secure their financial futures?

In the "hard sell" process at Gambling With Your Money, Inc. and other Wall Street casinos, buyers make decisions based on emotion rather than on information that they understand and that fits into their pre-determined needs and boundaries. Even though they think they understand the information given by the bookie, what happens when what they are given is misinformation?

How many people do you see at the mall buying supplemental nutritional pills because of mass marketing in health magazines and TV infomercials or on the advice of their "health advisor," Dr. Neighbor? Do you think they've consulted their doctors or health care professionals about what their actual nutritional deficiencies are? Likewise, we all know a person who got too excited about a refrigerator on the showroom floor of Best Buy and bought it on emotion only to realize that his new fridge doesn't fit into the designated spot in the kitchen? He was overwhelmed by the sight of the ice dispenser on the appliance, the sales talk of the sales associate, and the 15%-off coupon he found online. What a deal! Unfortunately, he let his emotions get the best of him and forgot to do the basic research on what size refrigerator would actually fit in his house!

Remember that the Wall Street salesperson has to create the fear in you that if you don't buy his product, then you will lose money or miss the boat on the gains.

Even if you suggest to him that you are not interested in the product, he will try to convince you that you are wrong and that you really need this investment in order to secure your retirement future.

That's the "hard sell" process. They're coming at you unsolicited by phone, dinner workshop invitations, or direct mail advertising to sell you stock and bond funds or "variable" annuities ... but they're really selling you out because you have no game plan to deal with the onslaught of information that you're not sure will work for you. But I have got a new game plan for you!

At Grace Advisory Group: Tax and Retirement Specialists, you'll discover that we've created a system that uses a "buy when ready" process. "Buy when ready" means that you are doing things with a plan versus no plan at all. When you come into our "store," you'll already have a plan based on your core values, the things that make you happy and content, and your investment parameters. Your plan objective will most certainly be to keep your money safe while growing your investments for retirement. If you didn't have this plan, you wouldn't have come to us in the first place. You'd be like those people standing outside Gambling With Your Money, Inc. or one of its many competitor casinos, waiting for the doors to open and waving your checkbook at the first bookie you see. That's not you.

The problem that exists in the Wall Street "hard sell" process is that most people don't possess the knowledge, time, and financial aptitude to discern what investment options lines up with their parameters of knowledge, understanding, and control. Nor do their well meaning friends, neighbors, or family members. People need the opportunity to educate themselves at their own pace about their financial goals rather than having a stranger tell them what they need or do not need before they're fully ready to make that important decision.

Our process begins with a familiarization process acquired through this book, the gracetax.com website, the workshops we hold at Ruth's Chris or Shula's Steakhouses, my weekly radio show "Retire with Grace," or by having our tax professionals prepare your tax return and the in house or referral attorney we recommend to make sure all your estate planning documents are up to date for our special "referral client" low fee. In this way, you gain the information on the strategies and products available to help you decide if our system works with your pre-determined life goals for you and your family.

We are proponents of using the cutting edge technology available to you in this process of familiarization. Do you still get off the highway to use a phone booth to make an emergency call? Do you still drive to the library and look up information on microfiche? Do you still contact your friends primarily by writing a letter and spending 44 cents on a stamp?

We find, however, that most people still insist on face-to-face interaction when it is time to create a personalized retirement plan and to review the plan designed specifically for their needs and sign the appropriate forms for the IRA transfer and account applications.

So what's it going to be? Will you call up a brokerage house like Gambling With Your Money, Inc. for the "hard sell" process, or will you visit our office for the "buy when ready" process?

Let's review. If someone who has not read this book calls up a brokerage house and says that they need some advice, what kind of advisor are they going to get? Will it be an experienced income tax and secure retirement specialist from Grace Advisory Group: Tax and Retirement Specialists, informed by decades of experience in retirement, tax, and real estate planning? Or will it be a Wall Street bookie ready to peddle some risk options off the casino's gaming menu? The bookies can help you answer some basic questions, but they have not in the past nor are they now able to put together a plan that will keep your hard-earned money safe.

If you are concerned about safety, the bookie's usual option for you is a balanced fund, long-term corporate bond fund, or a government securities fund. A balanced fund is essentially a mutual fund that consists of a combination of supposedly conservative stocks (an oxymoronic term at best) and safer bonds; in theory, a balanced fund is less risky than a mutual fund that consists solely of stocks. But what these brokerage house salesmen are recommending to you is putting lipstick on a pig (the phrase they use to describe those investments … behind your back).

Balanced mutual funds dropped 30% in the recent downturn—not much different from most mutual funds that dropped over 50% at the March 2009 lows. It's like walking into a casino and instead of playing the dollar slots, the casinos have arranged for you to play nickel slots. You think, "Hey, I won't lose as much playing nickels compared to dollars, right?" Hardly. You often lose more money playing on those nickels slots than playing on the dollar ones—it just takes a little longer!

Likewise, you can lose just as much money investing in balanced funds as regular mutual funds depending on the allocation of your total funds; it's just a different game on the Wall Street casino menu. Those bookies are not going to recommend a fixed indexed annuity or CDs, which are safe alternatives—that's not what they're paid to do. The responsibility of the brokerage house salespersons is to keep your money in the casino of stocks, mutual funds and variable annuities so they can collect fees and commissions whether you make money or not.

Take one of my long-time friends as an example; he has $250,000 in a bond fund. Recently over lunch, I asked him to explain the basic features of the fund to me, but he couldn't. I asked him if there are any guarantees that his money will be safe, and he answered, truthfully, "I don't know." You and I both know the answer is probably not.

Sadly, his situation is like most Americans who have their money tied up in investments that they don't understand. They only bought into these investments because their brokers said to do so. I told him that if he can't explain to his thirteen-year-old daughter where his money is and if it is safe, he's in the wrong deal. My friend said to me, "You know, you're right!"

If you come to us for your retirement needs, then you are telling us that you can't afford to lose any more money and you want a secure and peaceful retirement. I've already told you about the systems I developed based on my forty-three years of real world experience. You expect from us an objective analysis of your wants and needs—followed by a safe solution. You didn't come to our office just to browse, did you?

chapter nine

Success Stories

There's a reason why some folks do not open their quarterly statements: The fear of seeing negative numbers on a page all started for them during that 20% stock market drop in July and August of 2008. When the drop occurred, people began asking, "What about the products I heard Bob and his team talk about on "Retire with Grace"? Maybe it's time I do myself a favor, and grab a lifeboat before the Wall Street ship sinks." Those who were smart enough to consider this visited us, and the rest was history. They have not lost one penny but have had steady guaranteed growth.

After the July/August 2007 fiasco, things only got worse for the next two years; the S&P Index would drop another 40%. Yet, my clients weren't feeling the loss one bit. From 2007 to 2009, many of my clients had account statements that showed an increase of 10 to 15% on their money without any decrease in principal. This increase included the bonus that insurance companies gave them from signing up for the annuities that I recommended. During the last two years, I would ask my clients, "Are you feeling pretty good about making money while protecting money?"

And they would answer, "I have $550k in my retirement account now. Had I kept my money in a mutual fund, I would have $370k today. So, yeah, I'm feeling really good!"

None of them had any losses on their retirement or any accounts we recommended over the last ten years! My clients followed my strategy of transferring money out of stocks, mutual funds and variable annuities into the safety of CDs and fixed annuities and my advice to extract money from their houses in the form of mortgages, home equity loans, and reverse mortgages to create liquidity. I showed them how to take advantage of the arbitrage system by taking out a mortgage at one rate of interest, investing the money to earn a higher rate of returns, and keeping the difference. As a result, if they ever come across an emergency like a job layoff or disability, they will have money in their pockets to take care of it. They won't have to go to the bank and beg to borrow their own money because the banker doesn't think they can repay it.

I also deterred my clients from making bad decisions for their retirement funds. One of my clients was tempted to buy a house in foreclosure down the street in Gulf Harbour for a quick "fix & flip" as seen on TV. I told him, "Don't do it." I knew my client needed to keep money liquid and not put it into a risky investment.

I teach my clients to keep three to six months of income liquid in CDs or government bonds so they can handle any unforeseen issues in their lives. If that client had put his retirement money into buying another home without the knowledge, understanding, and control necessary to survive an overheated real estate market, he would have thrown money away and reduced his life expectancy from the ensuing stress.

In the following, I'd like to share with you some stories about the success my clients have achieved.

Betty Funds Her Retirement Travels

Betty came to see me when she was seventy-three years old. When her husband died eight years earlier, she had over $2 million in her account. By the time she came to Grace Advisory Group: Tax and Retirement Specialists, she'd lost all of it but half a million dollars. She'd trusted various advisors who put her in stocks and bonds that went down. Way down.

When she came in to my office, I asked her about her goals and her fears. Betty replied, "I have a house up north and a house down here in Naples. What I'd really like to do is travel. But I'm afraid I can't afford to."

"But Betty," I said. "You've got half a million in your account." She shrugged and said, "I'm still afraid I'll run out of money!"

Statistically, this is one of the biggest fears today's retirees face. They're not afraid of dying too soon, but living too long. In other words, they don't want to outlast their retirement funds!

So we worked with Betty to set up a Sequential Income Portfolio System that gave her $30,000 a year. That was non-qualified money—not from an IRA or 401(k). Because of the exclusion ratio on the annuity (an IRS law), she only paid taxes on about $1,000 of that $30,000. Her total tax was about $250 a year.

As our advisors were working on putting this program together, we received a call from Betty's son, who didn't hesitate in telling us his attorney was vehemently opposed to annuities. We conferenced in the attorney who gave us the laundry list of all the reasons why annuities fixed annuities were "horrible" and "no good"—the same lines Wall Street has been feeding wealthy people for years.

Fortunately, Betty's son had her best interests at heart. He honestly thought that annuities would sap her retirement fund and cost more money than they were worth. Once we explained to him the way it actually worked, he changed his tune. He knew his mother needed the income, and he understood that the tax benefit was substantial. After talking to us, he encouraged her to do it. She signed the paperwork that afternoon.

The uninformed attorney was still opposed. Being an attorney myself, I can vouch for the fact that they do not teach you anything about annuities or retirement planning in law school nor in CPA school. When a professional is asked advice about a subject they are not fully educated on the only safe and face-saving answer is don't do it. That answer more often than not does not serve their client's best interest.

Betty called me the next day. She had just booked a trip up north to see her grandkids.

"Thanks to you," she told me, "it looks like I'll get to travel after all!"

Thomas Safeguards a Portion of His $20 Million

A few months ago, I had a visit from Thomas, a very successful entrepreneur with a net worth of over $20 million. His son was a portfolio manager at a major investment bank in New York.

Five minutes into our meeting I said, "I have to be honest, Tom. What are you doing here? Why aren't you down in Naples with the marble pillars and high rollers?" I figured someone with that kind of money and a son on Wall Street was looking for a lot more risk than I was willing to offer.

"I've been listening to you on the radio for three months now," he said. "I like what you say about safety."

Turns out Tom didn't want to trust all of his future to the casino. He wanted at least some of the money he earmarked for his retirement to grow in a safe, controlled environment. He was mostly concerned about providing his wife and himself a "guaranteed" base which would then allow the balance of his assets to do what they will.

Tom was seventy-two and his wife was sixty-eight. He was in great shape and had income from his former employment. "I don't need this income for another six to eight years," he told me. "But I want to design a program where, no matter what happens … if I quadruple my $20 million or lose every penny of it … I'll know that I have enough annual income to maintain my and my wife's lifestyle no matter what. It sounds like you can guarantee that, right?"

I grinned. "Absolutely."

So I designed a program that is contractually guaranteed to give Tom and his wife a lifetime income, at any point in the future when they're ready to take it. Now Tom is free to play with the rest of that $20 million, all the while knowing he's got a guaranteed income waiting for him the moment he bites into his first slice of retirement party cake!

The Son Who Forfeited His Inheritance

I met Nancy three years ago when she came in with her husband, Greg. Greg was eighty-two and battling dementia, and consequently he didn't have a clear grasp of their finances. Nancy, on the other hand, was seventy-nine and sharp as a whip.

They had just short of $1 million in their retirement fund—$980,000, all in the stock market. I saw how much risk they were exposed to and put a plan together that would increase their income by over 35%. With SIPS as the founding principle, the plan eliminated all the risk, reduced their taxes, and guaranteed a lifetime income. It also locked in better interest rates, which meant there would be plenty of money left over for their kids.

Nancy was excited about the program. She'd been listening to my radio show for months and believed wholeheartedly in my approach. But unfortunately, Nancy's son wasn't quite as gung-ho. Les was a photographer in

Georgia who didn't have a strong background in finances. He took one look at the plan and thought his parents were being milked. He hated fixed annuities and told his mom to reverse the paperwork and put their money back in the stock market.

So Nancy came to me and, very apologetically, requested that we reverse everything we had done thus far. I gave them all their money back, shook hands, and wished them good luck.

That was three years ago—in 2008. I know they lost money between 2008 and 2009, probably more than half of that $980,000. They are still losing money today. The real irony is that the ignorance of their son not only cost *them* money … it cost him money, too. The inheritance he could have had waiting for him was decimated when the market crashed.

I've had clients in my office who have lost substantial sums in the market and are literally in tears. They had their 401(k) plans and no options to move their money to safe places. Right around the time they retired, the market took a hit. Many of them had $1 or $2 million and lost 30-50%. They either had to keep working or go out and get a part-time job. These folks were just heartbroken.

Fortunately, we've been able to give many of those people peace of mind. Now they sleep better at night knowing that, despite the losses they've suffered, they have a guaranteed lifetime income that nothing else can provide.

Sam and Sarah Take a Stroll

Sam and Sarah, both in their mid-seventies, came to one of my workshops five years ago. Over a delicious dinner of filet mignon and buttermilk mashed potatoes, they decided everything I was saying made a lot of sense and they were tired of gambling with their hard-earned cash.

At the time they had $400,000 in their retirement fund, and nearly 100% of that money was in stocks and bonds. They wanted to safeguard that money against potential fluctuations in the market, and they were eager to guarantee an income that would last the rest of their lives.

So we took the money out of the market and invested it in multiple laddered fixed annuities using SIPS. When many of Sam and Sarah's friends lost hundreds of thousands of dollars a couple years later, Sam and Sarah did not lose a cent.

Recently, Sarah stopped by my office to say hello.

"You know, my husband used to spend hours every day on the computer," she said. "He'd watch the market go up and down, up and down. It was awful. I couldn't get him away from that screen. He was glued to it, watching our money rise and fall, worrying about what might happen to our retirement future.

"Today it's a totally different story. We're out playing golf or bringing the grandkids down to see us. We take the boat out and go fishing. We go on long strolls through St. Armands Key and we don't have to worry about whether or not we can afford a new hat or scarf!"

Sam and Sarah know that, next month, they'll have another check in their account. Even if the account value goes to zero, that income will never stop. What other kind of investment gives you that sense of security? Stocks, bonds, mutual funds—when that money is gone, it's gone. The value is finite. But a properly designed Sequential Income Portfolio System using several layers of fixed annuities means a guaranteed lifestyle, no matter how long people live.

"It sounds like you're both enjoying life," I said to Sarah.

She nodded. "That's exactly what we're doing. Sam worked for forty-five years to arrive at the big day when he could finally relax and enjoy what he'd accomplished. Before we met you, he couldn't relax because he was still in the working paycheck mode. Now we're in retirement paycheck mode, living the life we always dreamed of!"

She gave me a big smile. "And all thanks to you and your team!"

Four Strategies for Successful Relationship Building

So how do the relationships between client and Grace Advisory Group: Tax and Retirement Specialists differ from what goes on in the Wall Street casino? I'm glad you asked! I have four strategies for Client Relationship Management that made the success stories that you just read possible.They are *Education*, *Evaluation*, *Implementation*, and *Preservation*.

Let's first discuss **Education**. My clients found us; we didn't hunt them down. They attended an educational workshop, visited our website, read about us in an interview in the media, or were referred to us by satisfied clients. The SIPS program and the fundamental beliefs of our company resonated in their hearts. So in the first stage of our relationship with our clients, I educate them about safe investments and about the system of risk on Wall Street.

The second stage is the **Evaluation** of the client's investment goals, parameters, and their lives in a broader sense. We want to help people discover a personalized strategy for their money that fits in with their goals and values. For example, a father makes $200,000 a year and is highly taxed. He has to figure out how to put four kids through college in the future, including giving them the option of going to private colleges. How is he going to do that without compromising his retirement future? How do his kids' educational expenses fit in the picture with his retirement security? At Grace Advisory Group: Tax and Retirement Specialists, it's very important for us to develop a retirement plan that incorporates all the pieces of a client's life.

Retirement planning is similar to the art of interior design. The designer has to make the wallpaper fit with the furniture and overall decor of the house. If the owners of the home are a conservative couple that listens to opera all the time, the designer shouldn't recommend polka-dot wallpaper that clashes with their dark-hued sofas, right?

In order to make our investment recommendations fit in with the lifestyles and dreams of our clients, I ask them during the initial evaluation: "Pretend it is three years from now; what do you want to see happen with your finances, career, and personal life that would make you feel good about your progress in those areas?" This question gets them thinking about their goals and values and not about the products I can offer them. In turn, their answers give me a better idea of their parameters and dreams, so that my team and I can recommend to them the right financial products for their retirement. Remember how we talked about how important it is for people to know their limits? It's just as important for their financial advisor to know his clients' limits. Otherwise, how can we create the right plan for them?

The third stage is **Implementation** or execution of the financial plan. We prepare the plan and revise it as desired by our client. At this stage, we put it into operation.

Finally, the fourth stage is the **Preservation** of our client relationships and their assets. We are constantly developing ways to give our clients up-to-date information about the financial environment. It's one of the reasons I host a weekly radio show—the information I share on "Retire with Grace" is a great way to keep my clients informed.

Lack of focus is the surest way to kill the planning that will achieve your dreams. It is of paramount importance that our clients are educated and reminded of their desire to stay the course in their solution, so that they aren't tempted to return to the Wall Street casino when people around them start bragging about how much they won at the "tables." I need to constantly remind them of what happened in 2007-2011, 2000-2003, 1991-1994, 1987, 1982, and even back in the early 1970s.

Client relationships are very important to me, and I want to make sure that my advice is available to them whenever they need it. People need to be reminded that gambling is an attitude that permeates American society. Betting is everywhere: sports, investments, and even odds on who is voted off reality TV shows! If that's your idea of entertainment, fine, but don't let it cross over into the way you think about managing your money!

Okay—now you've heard our clients' success stories and our successful philosophical approach to investing and relationship building. **What are you waiting for?** It's time to leave your broker with the **"it's not you, it's the uncertain economy"** break-up line and visit us to begin your own success story.

It's not your broker or even the firm. It's simply the market. The market goes up and the market goes down, and nobody—not you, your broker, your advisor, or the firm—can predict the future. There is *no* warning model. We are all only historians.

You've retired or are about to. You get your gold watch. You mall walk, but you've only got one tennis shoe on. You've not switched your financial planning to retirement (preservation and distribution) mode. Why? Because your advisor does not want to lose their paycheck. They get paid for putting your money at risk.

It should be all about you. Stop the bleeding. Move to safety, peace of mind, and a guaranteed lifetime tax-protected income that will last as long as you do, not just as long as the account does. "Retire with Grace."

I hope to be able to feature your success story in the sequel to this book. But that can only happen if you're willing to get out of the Wall Street casino … and stay out forever!

chapter ten

In Pursuit of a Successful Philosophy of Life

In this book I've talked a lot about knowledge. That's because knowledge is power.

I'm not just talking about financial knowledge. I'm talking about knowing yourself—who you are, what you want, and what's important to you.

Much of what we thought we knew has been stripped away over the last few years. Our faith in institutions, corporations, and in some ways humanity itself has been shaken to the core. The knowledge and wisdom we thought we had was shown to be a farce, and people like Bernie Madoff made us feel like fools. The Wall Street casinos made a killing on greed, and at the end of the day, we realized we'd been duped by pet rocks and hula hoops.

What is it we originally wanted? Wealth? Security? Happiness for our families and for ourselves? We weren't wrong to want those things. But to keep them safe in the future, we've got to change the way we invest our money and get serious about safety.

Remember how I talked about finding a "financial architect" in Chapter 2? A good financial architect helps you define boundaries for yourself, just like a blueprint of a house. It's your financial planner's job to find out what you want, what your goals are, and what you're afraid of. When a client comes into our office and says, "What can you do for me?", I don't have much to work with. It's like going to the doctor and saying, "Fix me." I can't prescribe a solution if I don't know where it hurts!

When I practiced law, there were three parts of a contract. There's the language (or terms), the length of time of the contract, and the money. Pick any two of those and I'll win the contract if I can pick the third.

I'm a big believer in straight talk. I tell my clients upfront: there's a string attached to everything. And the three strings attached to money are safety, liquidity, and rate of return. If you want safety and liquidity, you'll give up rate of return. If you want rate of return, you'll give up liquidity. Any institution that's going to give you a better rate of return is going to use your money for a period of time. That means you won't have unfettered access to it. In other words: you can't have all three. You have to pick and choose what you want and what's important to you. You also have to decide how much of your money goes where. What are you looking for in terms of liquidity and rate of return?

Money that's going to grow for you at a better rate of return has one big string attached, and it's called liquidity. That's why the SIPS program I developed isn't right for everybody. If you're somebody who needs all of your money to remain liquid, then annuities aren't right for you.

But if you're interested in safety, no risk, protection and security … if you want to increase your income, guarantee your principle, and eliminate fees … if you want to protect your estate and provide for your family … then I know we can help you.

And if you don't know whether or not you want these things, then I suggest you have a heart to heart with yourself. It's time to figure out what you want … which in the end will reveal who you truly are.

Defining Your Goals and Boundaries

Here's my philosophy of life that I like to share with other people: ***Know who you are and what your personal***

boundaries and goals are. Use that knowledge to evaluate your decisions about an investment, marriage, or career. If the information to make your decision is outside the parameters of your dreams or goals, you must decide accordingly. If you do what I just advised, you will have a better understanding of yourself and control of your life. What brings you the most fulfillment is an important key to your life. If you are trying to make decisions in which the consequences or results are more than likely outside your area of fulfillment, then don't make that decision.

Don't let the word "philosophy" scare you. I'm not here to tell you what the ultimate meaning of life is or how to live. Nobody has the key to life! I just want to share with you a couple lessons that I learned that have worked for me. Maybe, you'll find these lessons helpful for you.

Let's start with money. How should it fit into someone's life philosophy? I can't say what the perfect perspective on money is, but I know that for me, money is neither good nor bad. To me, money is just a tool. Money can be a tool for business development, a tool that builds a healthy retirement fund, or a tool to give back to society. For instance, I can't personally visit all the homeless shelters in Fort Myers to help the needy people in them, but I can donate money to these shelters. In this case, money is a tool for me to give back to the community.

There are all kinds of ways that our society looks at money. For example, money is associated with taxation. Most people hate taxes, but others see it as a necessary evil. Essentially, when we pay our taxes, we give the government money to protect us and care for us. Whether we associate money with donation or taxation, in my opinion, it's just a tool to help society run.

There are also people who hoard money with a selfish and greedy mindset. They don't believe in the principle of sowing and reaping. All they know is to accumulate money and never use it to bless other people. At the end of their miserly lives, all they will have is a vault full of money and a garage full of cars without any beneficiaries to appreciate them for sharing their wealth. If those scrooges don't make a decision about how to reposition their money to benefit others, then the government is going to make the decision for them (through taxation), and they will, ironically but inevitably, lose control of their riches. They'll become philanthropists against their wills, and their beneficiaries will be the Pentagon, 300,000,000 Americans they've never met before, and a whole bunch of government programs they probably spent their whole lives screaming against.

But there are a number of very wealthy people like the Rockefeller, Carnegie, and the Rothschild families who know the importance of charitable endeavors when it comes to money. To them, money is not just a tool for business; it is also a tool to give back to society.

Many people grew up with the notion that those with extreme wealth obtained their wealth dishonestly. For instance, the story was that Henry Ford got rich because he exploited his workers. Rockefeller made money because he ruthlessly controlled the railroad transportation of oil, and Bill Gates steamrolled start-up companies with his monopoly in the tech industry.

These stories about how rich guys made their wealth might be half true and half false. The sad thing is many people overlook the fact that those guys have given much of their wealth to charity. Gates has the Bill and Melinda Gates Foundation that works on causes like AIDS research. Rockefeller and Vanderbilt both have universities named after them for the support they provided education and research. Carnegie is a legendary name in American philanthropy. These successful people were successful because they could let go of their money and put it to use in a charity or a worthwhile investment that reaped benefits.

For me, a life philosophy about money is ultimately tied to the philosophy of giving and sharing your wealth. Money is a good tool if it helps you share your blessings with others. It's essential to look at money not only as a tool to buy or invest in things but also a tool to give back to your community. That way, you engage in the principle of sowing and reaping. You are not only helping others, but you are benefiting from the joy of helping fellow human beings. Remember that a true measure of a person is not how much he accumulates over his lifetime but how much he gives. The golfer Lee Trevino had a line I love: "What you take with you is what you leave behind."

Now, I'm not saying to give your money to just anybody or any organization to fulfill a life philosophy of giving. My philosophy of knowledge, understanding, and control still applies for charitable donations and bequests. You have to know what organizations help causes that are important to you, and you have to understand how they will use your money to further that cause. This allows you to exert control over how your charitable dollars are spent. If I find out that the organization to which I am looking to donate is funding things that I don't believe in or is exploiting their funds, then I won't donate. I'll just move on to another more effective organization.

I always do research before putting my money into something, and I encourage my clients to do the same. What part of the money they raise goes to the mission, and what part goes to salaries, fancy offices, luxury travel, and other perks? It can be shocking to discover just how "off mission" some charitable organizations can be. For all these reasons, it's important for me in an interview with my clients who want to donate to charity to find out what they are passionate about, what their causes are, and which charities they are familiar with before they write a check to a random organization.

If you are going to think of money as a tool in life, think of it as an arc that describes the path of an arrow. What's the target? How does the money travel along that arc—how does it get to where it's going? Use your money wisely by doing research on how to spend and protect it most effectively. Don't just throw cash into any investment or charitable organization before you see its fundamentals. Control the arc of your charitable spending and investing. Strike only when ready. Otherwise, you will shoot blindly, miss your target, and might even end up hurting someone. One caution—please don't get caught up in the paralysis of analysis. Seek the help of trusted competent credentialed professionals.

What Holds You Back from Success?

Let's turn now to a brief discussion of how success and failure fit into one's life. Some people are scared of success. Why? I can tell you the answer from personal experience because like many people, I've been afraid of success. Some people are afraid of the *responsibility* that comes with being successful. They think, "When I'm at the top, will I always do the right thing? Will I be judged correctly? Will I become a hypocrite? Will people hate me because I'm successful? Will it mess up my kids?"

In answer to those people's worries about being the next Trump or Buffett, I say this: Know who you are. Know your limits as we discussed at the outset of this book. Do your due diligence on your decisions. Ask questions like "Does this decision align with my values?" If you take this approach, success should not be worrisome to you. You'll handle success just fine. If you make your best effort to make the right decisions, you will often do the right thing no matter how successful you are.

In addition, you *should* be thinking about bringing forth success in your life. Otherwise, you are like the farmer who throws seeds haphazardly into the field without any goal of returns. That farmer will starve his family. You cannot go through life without wanting to be successful at the things you do. The desire to be successful gets things accomplished. Sitting there and doing nothing for fear of success doesn't get anybody anywhere.

There's also the fear of failure. This fear comes from the lack of faith in yourself or in the world. This fear is self-destructive and prevents you from accomplishing the things that you want. I've seen kids fail in their classes just so they do not qualify to play in a sports team. They are afraid that once they make the team, they would disappoint their parents if they ever lose a game. Failure isn't an outcome in these cases; it's a deliberate *strategy* to avoid an even worse outcome.

It's not only kids who have this fear; adults have it too. Someone might hold on to his money too tightly and not invest in a house that his wife wants for fear of losing money. He can afford the house given his financial situation, but he just doesn't do it. He lacks faith in the economy and in his ability to invest. In the end, his wife leaves him for his fear of failure. Therefore, the fear of failure can lead to decisions that produce destructive results. Fear of failure can bring failure in its wake.

If fear of failure is something that troubles you, as long as you are pursuing the good of the people in your life or the causes you care about, you shouldn't submit to the fear. For instance, you should not decline a job for fear of failing at it if this job could feed your family. Besides, who would hire you if they didn't think you are were competent enough to do the job? The fear of failure, like the fear of success, is debilitating. In order to get over these fears, you need to focus on the people you care about and what you can do for them instead of focusing on the fears themselves. Then there's the question of making decisions and the fear of making decisions, which we call procrastination. Recently, I came across an article titled "Thorough Research Creates Effective Decisions." I believe in the message of those words. Don't let anyone rush you into a decision before you have a chance to research the different aspects of the decision. Buying a refrigerator? Don't grab your wallet before you figure out what size fridge could actually fit in your kitchen or else you might end up returning your new appliance—not to mention the eye-rolling you'll get from your spouse. Don't be hurried into a decision on anything in life based on the perception that the opportunity will never be there again. As I stated earlier, life is full of thousands of new opportunities.

Be patient in your decision-making. In time, patience will reveal any kind of deception going on in a situation. For example, if you are going to invest in a new business venture, wait a little while before you actually put in money. During this time, you might find that the partners in this business venture are inept or that there is something wrong with their business model. Having patience will save your money from going down with a flawed investment. Patience will also save you time. A patient person doesn't have to use extra time to fix mistakes that he made from his hurried decisions. Measure twice and cut once. It's old advice, and it's still effective.

I stressed the "buy when ready" principle in a previous chapter because I know patience and research is important for any kind of decision. You should only jump into an investment or donation when you have done your due diligence (talking to people, looking at statistics, and so on) for that investment. The most important thing you can do when doing due diligence is "know thyself." Know what your financial situation is and how much money you can afford to give, lose, or reasonably gain. If you do that, your investment decisions will yield much better financial results. Based on the preparation that went into your decisions, you can look forward to achieving your desired outcome. You can better predict the results of your decisions by determining how much effort you put into your decisions. Or to put it simply, don't play darts when you're figuring out your life.

Moreover, one decision can teach you about another. One failed decision can lead to a successful decision. For instance, some of my greatest successes came from failures from certain situations. A loss can teach me to train in a different way or to train harder. Defeat doesn't hobble successful people. They take the licking, learn their lessons, and move on.

Develop a Uniform Philosophy

As you have probably noticed by now, my philosophy of life consists of three elements: **knowledge, understanding, and control**. It definitely makes it easier when you have a philosophy that is consistent all the way through, from your investments to your personal life. When I repeatedly use the term "control," I do not for a minute believe that we have any semblance of absolute control over things in our lives such as health and random things that just happen as a result of living in a world of dysfunction. I am basically using the word *control* for faith—**faith in whatever higher power you choose as the foundation for your personal philosophy of life.**

Let me give you an example of what I mean: You have never driven a car before and are learning the various features and functions of the vehicle. You desire to learn how to stop the car and to control how that happens. Well, you need **knowledge** of what stops a car, **understanding** of that knowledge to put it into action, and now you have the **control** to do what is necessary to stop the car. However, if you don't take the necessary action of faith (your control of the action of stepping on the brake), the car won't stop, no matter how much knowledge and understanding you have of the process.

Faith is **A**ction (control) based on **B**elief (Knowledge) sustained by your **C**onfidence (Understanding) that what the owner's manual said concerning how to stop the car is true—**the ABC's of Faith**, if you will.

What's this have to do with money, you ask? Well, if you do your homework and come to the conclusion that you're done gambling with Wall Street and with your financial future, and you come to an understanding that this approach will work for you; then you now control your future by taking the appropriate action of getting out of risk and into safety. It's that simple!

With your money in guaranteed safe financial investments, you would make about 6-8% average returns on your income account each year into the future. Sometime in the future, your buddy might tell you that he made 30% returns that year. Then he gives you the "look" and asks, "What are you doing with just 6-8% a year? You need to get back in the stock market. What are you, a chicken or something?" Your faith in your decision to use our recommendation will allow you to politely brush his suggestion away because you are fully confident that you made the right decision. Besides, if you average your buddy's gains in the stock market over the past ten years, his gains are probably negative even though he can brag about his 30% for one year. Maybe you have to be a chicken to lay the biggest nest egg!

One of my favorite song writers and performers, John Mellencamp, has a song with the message: "**You have to believe in something, or you will fall for anything.**" If you don't believe in anything else, at least believe in yourself to do the right things in escaping the Wall Street casino for a system of security and contentment.

The Next Generation

We've talked about you long enough. Now let's talk about your kids for a moment. Specifically, let's talk about raising children and how to leave our wealth to them. In sharing money with your children, you have to choose to partner up with them or to enable them. Let me illustrate the difference between partnering and enabling with the example of the Rothschild family.

The Rothschilds are a family of merchant bankers in Europe. As merchant bankers, they accumulate their wealth with the arbitrative system: They pay their customers X amount of interest for their deposits in the bank and loan money out for a higher interest rate. In the late 1700s, Mayer Rothschild, the patriarch of the family, had five sons. He needed to figure out a way to have his sons all take part in the family business and share the family wealth. He decided to put each son in a major

European capital to be in charge of the family business in those locations. With this arrangement, he taught his children responsibility by making them partake in the family business operations rather than just allowing them to eat of the fruit without any input or effort.

If any of the Rothschild sons wanted money from Dad, they had to *borrow* from the family bank. They couldn't say, "Dad, I need money" and expect the money to be handed to them; they had to write out a business plan for the money they wanted with an objective, details about the course of business, and how they were going to repay the loan in the future. If the kids wanted the money, they had to earn it. With this kind of discipline and the sense of responsibility that Mayer Rothschild instilled in his children, their family's banking dynasty survives to this day.

Mayer Rothschild was successful in distributing his wealth to his heirs and ensuring his family fortune would last into the future. He was able to do that because he partnered with his children by giving them a piece of the family business to manage responsibly.

In contrast to the Rothschilds, let's look at the example of the Vanderbilt family. Cornelius Vanderbilt was a highly successful businessman who amassed enough wealth in the late 1800s to donate a million dollars to Central Tennessee College, which is now Vanderbilt

University. Mr. Vanderbilt left money to his descendants with no game plan or strings attached. In other words, he enabled his children to use his wealth without them earning the money.

Recently at the 125th reunion of the Vanderbilt family at Vanderbilt University, the descendants of Cornelius Vanderbilt realized that not one of them at the reunion was a millionaire. One of the Vanderbilt heirs said that he saw his father and his grandfather, the direct heirs of Cornelius, have their relationships and marriages broken because of the money issues they had.

Remember the earlier discussion of the futility of pursuing happiness from money? See the difference between enabling your children and partnering up with your children when it comes to family wealth? Money is a tool, not an end. Happiness based on a contented heart is the goal, not a vast sum of money handed to you without a plan or system in place.

When my kids were teenagers of driving age and were leaving the house, I would ask them, "Where are you going?" And they would give me an annoyed look and say, "Out."

Then I would respond, "Well, while you are 'out,' make sure you are driving the car. I don't want you to be the passenger in someone else's car late at night."

The reason I insisted on this was because I had knowledge, understanding, and control on how I taught my kids to drive a car and to do it defensively and responsibly. I didn't have the same confidence in other kids' training or skills. Because they demonstrated to me during their first year of driving that I taught them well, I had much peace of mind knowing that if they screwed up, they would be responsible for the consequences, not somebody else's kid. And my faith in them has produced good results!

From Money to Marriage

Now let me give my two cents about the marriage relationship. Sometimes, spouses are not on the same page on certain issues in life, such as where to invest for retirement or where to send the kids for pre-school. As if the conflict between two people wasn't enough, we might also have the grandparents chipping in an opinion or two. As a result, we might have four different outlooks on one issue. How do we keep competing outlooks on issues like money, raising kids, and career choices from overwhelming a marriage?

Obviously, in the courting process before marriage, people don't discuss money matters because talking about money can be a deal breaker. In the back of our minds, we might fear, "What if the other person strongly disagrees with my financial or political perspective? Or what if they realize I don't have as much money as they had hoped?" So we keep silent about money before marriage. Keeping silent in the courting process about finances is not always a good thing because a wife might find out a husband's real opinion about how to earn and handle money too late in a marriage.

In a marriage (and only when people ask for my opinion!), I advise that either the wife or the husband (but not both) take charge of the decision-making in certain aspects of life like household management, business planning, and so on. As a result, the wife or the husband who has not been designated the implementer of the plan can be in the role of counselor on the specific issues. In this way, they are a team, but the responsibility to implement the plan falls on one party who is gifted in the administration of the family budget and financial bookkeeping.

I don't believe in joint banking accounts. I do believe in joint savings accounts, but the family budget needs to be handled out of one checking account. You need to know what each of you earns, how much tax withholding and contribution to retirement savings needs to come out of each paycheck, and then each of you put your pro-rata funds into the monthly budget account. You each need to agree on how much each of you can spend (without having to ask your partner) on the basics for the wife (nails, hair, monthly needs of kids' activities, etc.) and for the husband (recreational activities like golf, going to ball games with friends, grooming needs, etc). However, there is nothing sadder in my experience of counseling families than seeing one party or the other having to answer to the other on every single dime that is not excessive or outside the ordinary for one to enjoy life.

And men—-if your wife doesn't work or works part time, you need to realize that you need to give her a monthly, agreed-upon salary for her hard work in running your kingdom at home. Remember that if you don't get that fact now, her divorce attorney will help you understand it later!

Finally, there are certain decisions in a marriage that are very hard to make when we bring in the issue of money. For example, let's say a young couple who has been married for ten years lives in Sarasota with two kids. Their support system is here. One day, the wife's company wants her to move to Jacksonville and will pay her an extra $100,000 for doing so. If money is this couple's god, then the choice is obvious for them. If their values are attached to their support system in Sarasota, then they need to decline this offer. But what if the family has to move or the wife will lose her job?

Suddenly the decision becomes more complicated. In this case, in order to make the right decision, the couple has to examine their needs and their values. If they need the wife's income, then they will move. If they don't, they can stay in Sarasota, and the husband can be the sole breadwinner for a while. It is important to realize from this example that money cannot decide everything in a marriage. It is through careful examination of the values in a marriage that effective decisions are made.

I do investigative background research before most of my decisions in life whether about business, finances, health, technology, or my personal life. I let my knowledge become understanding, and I let that understanding become wisdom. When I apply my wisdom properly, I gain control of my health, wealth, and happiness. As I mentioned earlier in this chapter, control is really faith that this particular action that I'm about to engage in would give me this outcome the majority of the time. If I am unsure of the outcome of my actions, then I am acting out of stupidity or "blind faith."

Thorough research creates effective decisions! Your entire life hinges on the decisions you make.Your decisions will create tragedies or joy. Laughter or tears. Pain or pleasure. Don't let anyone rush you into any decision before you are prepared. Be patient, and adhere to the "Buy when ready" process not "hard sell." Remember that Patience is the weapon that forces Deception to reveal itself.

Understanding of knowledge is not only essential for our actions, but it is also important for connecting with other people. In order to develop meaningful relationships, you have to understand the areas on which you and the other person agree or disagree. Stupidity is when you marry someone you haven't fully understood and therefore don't completely trust, then wonder why it didn't work out. I'm very happy with my relationship with my wife and kids because I know and understand and accept them. This way I can minimize my mistakes when it comes to decisions I make in my relationship with them. **Trustworthiness** is the single most important trait that you must have to enjoy meaningful and fruitful relationships with our family, friends, and others in the community.

Understanding and trustworthiness are also paramount in the relationship between a financial advisor and his/her client. Some people are afraid to "fire" their financial advisors because they fear their advisors' feelings would be hurt. But they have to understand that their relationships with their brokers are purely professional, even if your broker happens to be your roommate from college.

If you need a little help, try giving a copy of our Certificate of Assurance to your advisor. If he or she is willing to sign it, great! Of course, in our experience, they never are.

Certificate of Assurance

I, ______________________________ (your Wall Street advisor), am recommending various Wall Street options for your retirement money. I am fully aware you are unwilling and cannot afford, at this stage in your financial life, to lose ANY portion of your retirement assets. Therefore, if you follow my recommendations and you lose any money, I will personally make up any losses so as to guarantee your peace of mind and assure that you and your spouse will never run out of money in retirement.

______________________________ ______________

Wall Street Advisor Signature *Date*

The decision to leave the Wall Street firm is a financial decision, not a decision about friendship. Unless your broker is willing to reimburse you for your recently devastated portfolio so that you can retire in the lifestyle you had hoped for, then it's a business relationship. And you need to make the necessary business decision that lines up with your desire for risk or safety. It's that simple!

chapter eleven

Some Final Thoughts

By now, you know me pretty well. You know what I believe about investing (saving). You know how I feel about risk in general and about the way the Wall Street casino peddles risk, taking advantage of investors' fear (and greed) and their desire to look good and sound cool at cocktail parties. You know how I feel about the importance of sleeping soundly at night because your money, retirement, and future are safe. You know my spiritual core and my thoughts about how money fits into a balanced life. You even know that I take my own advice.

Although we may have never met, I know a lot about you—simply because you've read this book all the way to the end. I know that you're a hard-working person who takes your responsibilities in life seriously—at work, at home, and in your financial life. I know that either you or people you know well have been burned by Wall Street and that you've witnessed tens or even hundreds of thousands of hard-earned dollars vanish once the music stopped. I know you've always believed there was a better way. I'd like to believe you've found it now.

Some people may never invest with me, and I understand that fact. You can't be all things to all people. As we've discussed, I'll never attract the get-rich-quick types, the people who go from infomercial to seminar, waving their credit cards at the "gurus" who may not know how to enrich you, but they sure know how to enrich themselves. The penny stock pickers, the day traders, the people who think they'll make a fortune trading stock options or buying and flipping foreclosures (at the same time that people who actually know something about real estate are going bust) … they're not in my sights, and I'm not in theirs.

But you're different. You're too smart to fall for the hype. I've deliberately written this book in a straightforward, down-to-earth, easy-to-understand manner because the concepts I've sought to share with you in these pages are exactly that: straightforward, down to earth, and easy to understand.

Risk is bad.

A loss is more dangerous to your overall financial health than a gain benefits you.

If you don't have understanding, knowledge, and control over your money, then someone else does. And they are more likely to make profits themselves than help you.

The market doesn't just go up. It goes down, and when it goes down, it takes the hard-earned money of many good people with it. The brokers live to sell another day, but you don't have another twenty years to make up for the money you can lose in a matter of months.

As an investment philosophy, **safety beats fear and greed every time**. It was true in King Solomon's day, and it's equally true in ours.

If you can't explain an investment to your twelve-year-old, then you shouldn't be making that investment.

Wall Street's system is for accumulating money … and it fails desperately at preserving and distributing it to the people who need it.

When it came time to take responsibility for the loss of trillions of dollars of investor wealth, Wall Street blamed everyone but itself. "Trust us," they said. But when the market collapsed, Wall Street's tune changed. It became, "You should never have trusted us."

You're probably thinking, "If this stuff is so obvious, why doesn't everybody preach it?" And by now, you know the answer. There's more money for Wall Street in keeping the status quo of tapping into people's fear and greed, so they can tap into their pocketbooks. A commission here, a fee there … it all adds up to money out of your account and into their pockets. Where do you think they get the money to pay themselves those obscene salaries and bonuses? From thin air? No, from hard-working people like you!

By now, you also realize just how passionate I am about working with people like you to protect your investment and keep it safe, so that you can count on your money now and in the future. It's never too late to have the retirement you always dreamed of. All you need to know is *How To Make Sure Your Money Lasts As Long As You Do!*, and the rest is history!

I hope this book has been valuable to you in solving your need of securing your retirement future, without Wall Street risk. Your intention to have your assets protected needs your action to do so. I invite you to contact me or one of my associates so we may continue the conversation. Feel free to visit our website at www.gracetax.com, or contact our main office at (239) 481-5550.

Is the road you're on leading you to the destination you want to go? If not, I look forward to helping you change course!

With best wishes for a safe, enjoyable, and financially secure retirement,

Bob

Robert E. Grace
JD, CLU, ChFC, CFEd®, RFC
Master Elite IRA Advisor ®